LIVING IN

DOWNTOWN INDY

LIVING IN
DOWNTOWN
INDY

by
Norm Crampton

Your Total Guide to
What's What & Where

Crampton Associates
Indianapolis

Living in Downtown Indy:
Your Total Guide to What's What & Where
Published by Crampton Associates
901 N. East St., Studio 2
Indianapolis, IN 46202-3425
317-341-3408
www.lvndntn@yahoo.com

Cover illustration by Chris Pyle
Cover and interior design by Sara Love

Notice of Rights

Distribution
For sales inquiries and special prices for bulk
quantities, please contact the publisher.

Limit of liability, disclaimer of warranty

ISBN: 0-9754020-0-5
Printed by Signature Book Printing, Inc.,
Gaithersburg, MD

Acknowledgments

Special thanks go first to the people who sat down with me and explained why downtown Indianapolis is becoming such a great place to call home. They are:

Bill Brooks, journalist, editor of *The Lockerbie Letter*
Bill Gray, executive director, Riley Area Development Corporation
Joe Everhart, real estate broker and old house makeover expert
Joan Lonneman, real estate broker, downtown booster
Leah Orr, sculptor, neighborhood activist
Susan Williams, CEO, Indiana State Office Building Commission,
    longtime resident of Chatham Arch
Tamara Zahn, president, Indianapolis Downtown, Inc.

Many thanks, as well, to IDI staff members Nicole Roberts and Susan McKenna for pointing me in the direction of good downtown data and offering suggestions on the manuscript. And to LeEtta Davenport, Community Relations Patrol Officer of the Indianapolis Police Department, for securing data essential to portions of Chapter 10.

The seating charts for sports and theater venues listed in Chapters 5 and 6 were provided with the special assistance of Matt Guay, Indianapolis Indians; Jeff Johnson, Pacers Sports & Entertainment; Heidi Mallin, Indiana Convention Center & RCA Dome; Justin Hart, Indianapolis Ice; Scott Tolley, Murat Centre; David Owens, Madame Walker Theatre Center; and the anonymous but very helpful box office staff at Indiana Repertory Theater, American Caberet Theatre, Phoenix Theatre, Theatre on the Square, and the Hilbert Circle Theatre, home of the Indianapolis Symphony Orchestra. Thanks to one and all.

Special thanks to artist Chris Pyle, who captured the spirit of downtown Indy in a dazzling cover drawing.

And finally, to graphic designer Sara Love, who orchestrated the entire design of this book from cover to cover and did so in great style, many thanks for your many talents and hard work.

—Norm Crampton

Table of Contents

Introduction
Big Urban Place with a Small-Town Heart **1**

Chapter 1
Finding Your New Home in Downtown Indy **7**

Chapter 2
Moving In and Hooking Up **27**

Chapter 3
Going Shopping **35**

Chapter 4
Eating Out **45**

Chapter 5
Cheering the Team **55**

Chapter 6
Show Time! **63**

Chapter 7
Staying Healthy, Top to Toe **77**

Chapter 8
Staying in Shape Downtown **87**

Chapter 9
Keeping a Car Downtown **95**

Chapter 10
Calling the Cops—or Your City-County Council Rep **99**

Chapter 11
Downtown Directory **107**

Chapter 12
Maps—Finding Your Way Around Downtown Indy **147**

Big Urban Place with a Small-Town Heart

This book is about discovering your new home base in the vital center of Indianapolis, Indiana. This book is your guide as you explore and get to know downtown Indy, decide where to live, and settle in. It shows you around your new neighborhood, introduces you to the wealth of fun and good times you can have downtown, prepares you for a few little challenges of downtown life, and confirms your good judgment in adopting downtown Indy as your new home address.

If you already live or work downtown, you know a lot about this neighborhood, at least your neck of the woods and your everyday routes. *Living in Downtown Indy* can help fill in details about downtown that are off your beaten path. It can show you new ways to get more out of life in a very special urban U.S. center that has everything you expect to find in a big city—classy stores and shops, great food, world-class entertainment, public spaces that you like to show off to visitors and make you proud to live here.

But downtown Indy is rare among American big cities because of another quality that residents know well. Beneath the veneer of downtown sophistication beats the heart of a small town. That's an unusual combination. You won't find it much in the Loop and hardly ever in Times Square (as they say, great places to visit but you wouldn't want to live there).

Feeling Friendly—and Safe

What does it mean to have the heart of a small town? It means mainly that you encounter friendliness and you feel safe. One quick way to measure these two important qualities is to observe how often strangers make eye-contact in downtown Indy. People feel safe enough in this downtown neighborhood to acknowledge one another, the way folks do in small towns. Acknowledging means momentarily locking eyes, and smiling. It's a beautiful thing. (You're skeptical? Try this: Walk around one block of downtown Indy, make eye-contact and smile at three or four people. See if you don't get smiles and hellos in return. That doesn't happen much in Chicago or New York.) Of course, when you adopt downtown as your home turf you begin to see familiar faces every day. And you bump into old friends all the time. That's how it works in a small town.

Another test of small town charm is to observe how car traffic acknowledges foot traffic, and vice-versa. Pedestrians in downtown Indy mostly observe the Walk-Don't Walk signals, a common courtesy. And motorists mostly grant walkers the right of way at marked crosswalks including the striped mid-block crossings on some downtown streets. For both parties—driver and walker—practicing this small-town courtesy generates an extraordinarily good feeling, the traffic equivalent of a nice big smile.

Downtown Indy also feels safe because it's clean. Sure, we have our moments of wind-whipped litter. But most of the time the sidewalks and streets are pretty well picked up, thanks largely to a broad feeling of responsibility that shopkeepers and building managers share concerning the looks of their neighborhood—taking pride in the appearance of "Main Street," another small-town thing.

An Inviting Place—and Walkable

The sense of security that you feel in downtown Indy comes, in part, from the way it's designed. The place is bright, airy, and built to human scale. Unlike the shadowy canyons of some downtowns (courtesy forbids naming names, but think of those other places you've been to recently), the center of Indianapolis is designed with broad streets and sidewalks that are simply inviting.

Downtown is orderly, neatly divided into four quadrants, each clearly labeled. Downtown is compact—and eminently walkable. In fact, its walkability probably explains more of the charm of downtown Indy than any other characteristic. For if you can walk a place, you can get to know it very well and make it your own. That may be a tough concept to understand while you're living in the suburbs and controlling your fate from the steering wheel of an SUV. But it all becomes crystal clear the first day you walk from Monument Circle to your downtown residence in 15 minutes or so—while your friends and colleagues are bumper to bumper on their way home to Johnson and Hamilton counties.

"Walking distance" really is a key idea about living downtown. When new residents of downtown Indy talk with old friends living in other places, they almost always report, "I can walk everywhere," or words to that effect. And it's true. Residents in apartments along the Upper Canal walk to games at Conseco Fieldhouse. Residents in the Chatham Arch neighborhood in the Northeast Quadrant walk to the RCA Dome in the Southwest Quadrant to cheer the Colts. And hundreds of downtowners really do walk to work every day from their homes throughout the downtown neighborhood. They discover that walking can be just as fulfilling as piloting a Hummer—and you get much better mileage.

Certainly a large part of feeling safe downtown is seeing uniformed police officers on patrol, on bikes (both pedal and Harley), and even on horseback. The Indianapolis Police Department's mounted force is one of the dividends of downtown life in a popular convention city, which Indy certainly is. The mounted patrol are hugely popular photo-ops for visitors and supremely effective managers of large crowds, a reassuring sight when you're having fun *en masse*. People like coming to national meetings in downtown Indy for the same reason that Hoosiers like living in downtown Indy—because the place looks and feels safe. For more on the topic of safety downtown, take a look at Chapter 10.

Defining "Downtown"

In this book, the neighborhood of downtown Indianapolis is the rectangle formed by I-65 on the north, the I-65/I-70 combo on the east, I-70 on the south, and the White River on the west. The little map shows you exactly where those boundaries are—the area measures 2 miles north to south and about 2.3 miles east-west.

Using the I-65/70 loop as the downtown boundary does exclude some very respectable neighborhoods that lie just the other side of the Interstate highways, like Fountain Square, down Virginia Avenue; and the Old North Side, running up toward 16th Street; and Cottage Home and Woodruff Place, over east near Arsenal Technical High School. Agreed—it's an outrageously arbitrary decision to exclude those fine places from the territory of "downtown." The only defense is that Fountain Square, Woodruff, Old North Side,

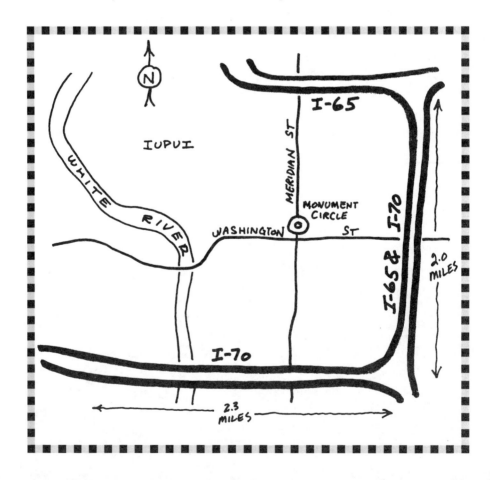

and other neighborhoods outside the "inner circle" all lie at the very edge or beyond what most people would think of as comfortable walking distance from Monument Circle, and because this book uses walkability as a prime measure of the good life when you call downtown your home—well, you get the point. But these limits on downtown are not cast in Interstate concrete. When the city paints bike lanes on downtown streets, it will be time to rewrite this definition of downtown Indy.

How To Use This Book

You don't have to read every page! *Living in Downtown Indy* is a *reference* book, a handy guide when you need specific information, like finding a video store, ordering a pizza, or getting your car serviced. The alphabetical Directory in Chapter 11 is designed to answer questions like that. And every entry in the Directory is keyed to a map—all the maps appear in Chapter 12. If you're simply curious about what's on the various blocks of downtown Indy, by all means spend some time in Chapter 12. Naturally, you'll want to find the street you live on and put a big red X on the map. To find your neighborhood and street, use the Map Finder on the last page of the book—it shows what page the various maps appear on.

Chapter organization follows a plan based on the assumption that you're new to downtown Indy. So, first things first: getting to know the neighborhoods and deciding where to live. That's the topic of Chapter 1.

Chapter 2 tells you how to connect to the various utilities and communications systems, including the electric and gas companies, and the cable and phone companies.

Chapter 3 talks about your shopping choices downtown.

Chapter 4 is your guide to eating out. You'll find restaurants organized by kind of cuisine, with notes about price, reservations, and the other essentials. The author's list of favorite restaurants also appears in Chapter 4.

Chapters 5 and 6 are your references to the entertainment scene in downtown Indy, with contact info for all the theaters, arenas, and other venues—including seating plans to help you order tickets.

Chapters 7 and 8 contain more lists and contacts for taking care of you and yours: dentists, physicians, workout studios, fitness programs, plus suggestions for walking and cycling downtown.

And speaking of getting around, Chapter 9 covers car care in downtown Indy plus suggestions about other modes of transportation, including your choices for getting to the airport.

Chapter 10 covers government services such as police and fire, as well as the names and numbers for your representatives on the City-County Council. Chapter 10 also covers the important topic of personal safety and compares crime rates in downtown Indy to the Hamilton County suburb of Carmel. The numbers may surprise you—and reassure you.

So, that's a quick look at what's in this book. Your comments, suggestions, and corrections are welcome. Send them to lvndntn@yahoo.com—and have fun getting to know downtown Indy!

Finding Your New Home in Downtown Indy

If you've already found your new home in downtown Indy—congratulations and welcome! You can skim this chapter so you know what it covers, for future reference. But if you're only starting to look around and figuring out what's where on the downtown scene, you may want to take a closer look at the sections ahead. In this chapter you can discover:

◎ How downtown Indy is organized, geographically speaking
◎ Where the residential neighborhoods are, what they're called, and a bit about their character
◎ Where to find the principal condominium and apartment communities plus some idea about amenities and cost
◎ Some examples of the cost of single-family, detached dwellings and townhouses

Chapter 1 and later chapters also contain a few sidebar comments by folks who know downtown Indy very well and have some perspectives to share with you.

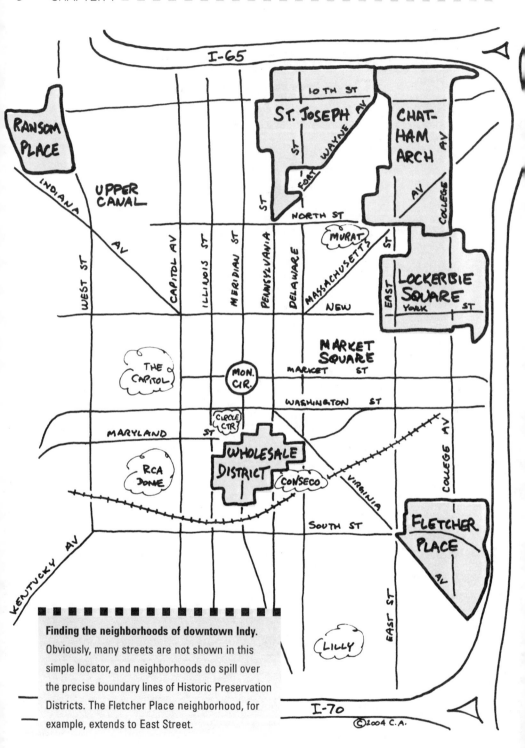

Finding the neighborhoods of downtown Indy.
Obviously, many streets are not shown in this
simple locator, and neighborhoods do spill over
the precise boundary lines of Historic Preservation
Districts. The Fletcher Place neighborhood, for
example, extends to East Street.

Getting to Know the Territory

Despite those maddening one-way and angle streets in downtown Indy, the city center really is easy to understand. Well, yes—when you're first cruising the territory it may take awhile for you to learn the one-ways so well that you can zip around downtown with your eyes closed, so to speak. But the city fathers and mothers have devised an organizational scheme to help you put every *other* part of downtown in its place—while you learn that Washington Street runs west, Maryland Street runs east, East Street runs south, and so on. That organizing idea is called The Quadrants. As the name suggests, there are four of them. If you're standing on the steps at Monument Circle facing north (in your best Sylvester pose), the Northeast Quadrant is on your right hand and the Northwest Quadrant on your left hand. Walk around to the south Monument steps, face south, and the Southwest Quadrant is on your right hand and the Southeast Quadrant on your left hand.

To show you how useful the quadrants are for organizing downtown info, here are some facts to remember, by the quadrants:

◎ The greatest variety and largest supply of residential housing in down-town Indy is in the Northeast Quadrant. More people live in the NE quadrant than any other (Census, 2000).
◎ The Northwest Quadrant contains most of the large apartment buildings.
◎ The Southeast Quadrant contains the fewest number of apartment units.
◎ The Southwest Quadrant (RCA Dome and beyond) contains the fewest number of residential units of any kind.

That's the big picture in a nutshell—or rather, a quadrant. See how easy it is to remember when you sort things by quadrants? Besides the quadrant signs at Monument Circle, additional signs are posted out in the quadrants at various crossroads, reminding you where you are and what's nearby. But remember, too, that everything you learn about downtown today is subject to change tomorrow. Downtown Indy is developing at amazing speed. Builders continue to break ground for new residences and announce plans to rehab old buildings into new condos and apartments. Also, there's talk about expanding the Indiana Convention Center and building a new sports arena to replace the RCA Dome, perhaps in the Southwest Quadrant. That could influence the development of additional residential units in the Southwest. But don't worry about keeping up to date. Once you're a member of the downtown community you'll become an expert—everyone is!

Another organizational device in downtown Indy is much older than the Quadrant scheme. It's called the Mile Square, and you may hear references to it when people talk about downtown. The Mile Square is the area bounded by North Street, East Street, South Street, and West Street; you can find those streets on the map at the beginning of this chapter. And it really is a square mile, or very close—on the author's odometer, the north-south distance clocks a bit under a mile. No big deal. What does matter and you might remember is that the phrase "Mile Square" sometimes is used loosely to describe the territory of downtown Indy, and that can be misleading. These days, "downtown" means at least the area enclosed by the Interstate wrap-around and the White River, which measures 2 miles north-south and about 2.3 miles east-west. Some people also include the Old North Side neighborhood—north of I-65 up to 16th Street—in their definition of downtown, but this book does not, for reasons explained in the Introduction.

Cruising the Neighborhoods

The map also is the place to begin your orientation to downtown and prepare to get well acquainted with the area. The map shows you the basic outlines and main features of downtown Indy, including:

- ◎ Monument Circle at the center
- ◎ The Mile Square streets—North, East, South, West
- ◎ The angled avenues radiating from the center like spokes— Massachusetts, Virginia, Kentucky, Indiana. They're called avenues, not streets, presumably because they serve bigger purposes than streets. For example, Massachusetts Avenue, or Mass Avenue as everyone calls it, is the "Main Street" of a thriving downtown neighborhood of restaurants, galleries, theaters, and specialty retailers. Indiana Avenue historically has served the same purpose and plans are afoot to revive some of its old glory.
- ◎ The neighborhoods of downtown that people call by name: Ransom Place, St. Joseph, Chatham-Arch, Lockerbie Square, the Wholesale

District, and Fletcher Place. Each one is described briefly in the following section of this chapter.

The outlines of the neighborhoods may look a little fussy, zigging and zagging. Those are the legal boundaries determined by property owners in cooperation with the Indianapolis Historic Preservation Commission. In everyday life, the communities are very informal and inviting—you don't need a passport!

Lockerbie Square

Lockerbie Square is a Victorian village—pretty as a postcard, historic, settled, prosperous, and proud. A Lockerbie address confers status that most other neighborhoods of downtown Indy do not. But Lockerbie has earned every bit of the recognition it receives today. Thirty-five years ago it was a backwater of downtown. Lockerbie was slowly falling apart, waiting, hopefully, for pioneers to come along and refresh the little urban village that James Whitcomb Riley described as "nestled away from the noise of the city and heat of the day." Riley, the celebrated Hoosier poet, made his home at 528 Lockerbie Street, a stunning Victorian structure—now a museum—that serves as the spiritual anchor of the neighborhood (see map **M-10**).

"Everyone thinks everyone in Lockerbie is rich," says Lockerbie resident Bill Brooks, a journalist

■ ■ ■ ■ ■ ■ ■ ■ ■ ■ ■ ■ ■ ■ ■ ■

Bill Brooks:

"Sure, we walk nearly everywhere…"

Journalist Bill Brooks lives in Lockerbie Square and, like many downtowners, walks to work. The following is excerpted with permission from an article he wrote in the November 2001 Lockerbie Letter.

"It's a Saturday morning in early October and you suddenly remember that the Circle City Classic Parade begins in less than an hour. The brightly colored trees sway in a gentle autumn wind, the sun shines brightly over your shoulder, and you feel like tapping your feet and swiveling your hips. No problem; a five-minute walk with a camper's chair and you've got a front-row seat for the best parade of this or any year. This is why we love living in Lockerbie Square, where we don't have to pay $7 to park when the Ribfest comes to town. That money can go, instead, toward calories and cholesterol. When we think of reasons for living downtown, we think often about our ability to walk. Or that we don't have to plan much ahead for a trip to the Indiana State Museum or a stroll on the Canal or an evening at the theater. Some of us love Lockerbie because—on the snowiest or coldest day of the year—we don't even need a coat as we make the five-minute trip from our own garage to the Nordstrom garage. Sure, we walk nearly everywhere, but there are special exceptions, such as a shoe sale on a rainy day."

and editor of the monthly *Lockerbie Letter.* "In fact we have a fairly eclectic neighborhood. What we have is a downtown small town where people walk their dogs and know each other."

And rise to the occasion, he might add. Lockerbie residents were the first downtowners to organize and carry out a restoration plan for their neighborhood, beginning with the designation of Lockerbie in 1967 as the first Indianapolis Historic Preservation District. Living in such a district has its pluses and minuses some people say. Status as a district means you abide by certain rules governing what you can do to your property, with the general aim of preserving the original architectural design as much as possible.

"You don't have the freedom to remodel your place or add certain outdoor amenities that strike your fancy," says Brooks. "If you paint your mailbox in cute designer colors or plop a hot-tub in the backyard, you may get a notice to cease and desist—and redo."

Though some folks may chafe at rules like that, the guidelines and restrictions are regarded as a key part of restoring historically significant neighborhoods to their old glory—and improving property values along the way. Recent real estate transactions in Lockerbie certainly confirm the money part: Many dwellings trade in the half-million dollar range. (For more details on what it means to live in a designated historic district in downtown Indy, please see Chapter 10.)

Almost entirely residential, Lockerbie contains a mix of housing including townhouses, condominiums (most notably, The Glove Factory), apartments, and the signature collection of single-family dwellings, many over a century old. The only remaining piece of Lockerbie to be developed is a large grassy block on the north side of Michigan Street between College and Park avenues. The Mormon Church had designs on the property a few years ago, but Lockerbie residents turned thumbs down.

When you look at Lockerbie, begin your drive-around on the only cobblestone street in Indianapolis—Lockerbie Street (see map **M-10**).

Fletcher Place

Fletcher Place is a diamond in the rough. Compared to neighborhoods north of Monument Circle, Fletcher Place, in the Southeast Quadrant, is inconsistent from street to street and edgy in spots. There are some tear-down candidates here, but there are some real gems, too, and lots of fixer-upper properties that should pay back nicely if you can buy low and wait a few years.

"People have dumped on Fletcher because they kind of think it's the stepchild of downtown neighborhoods," says real estate broker Joe Everhart. "But today's marginal or scary neighborhood is usually just about one press release away from becoming a really vibrant neighborhood—a finished neighborhood."

Everhart thinks one reason Fletcher trails other downtown neighborhoods is that it's practically invisible to the suburban commuter crowd. The heavy weekday traffic into downtown from Hamilton County, for example, never passes through Fletcher-land, and much of the traffic from Johnson, Hendricks, and Hancock counties also bypasses Fletcher. So the neighborhood doesn't get the exposure it deserves. Another problem is the ugly band of railroad tracks running across the south side of downtown Indy, and the forbidding dark underpasses that provide the only passage through. Neighborhoods on the north side of Monument Circle don't have to deal with a barrier like that. Still, Fletcher is happy home to numerous workers at the big employers on the south side of downtown—Eli Lilly & Co., Anthem, and Farm Bureau, for example.

When you look at Fletcher, take a look at the townhouses on Lord Street; the condos in Union Laundry Lofts Building, at 735 Lexington Avenue; the apartments at the old Calvin Fletcher School, at the southeast corner of Lexington and Virginia avenues; as well as single-family dwellings along Fletcher Avenue, Pine Street, and Greer Street, for example.

Fletcher Place offers a wide variety of housing and some real bargains. And it has a nice little neighborhood park with plenty of kiddie apparatus: Edna Balz Lacy Park, at East and McCarty streets, see map **M-23** and **M-29**.

Joe Everhart:

"We're very suburban in an urban setting"

Joe Everhart is a real estate broker with the Sycamore Group—and a veteran buyer-rehabber of downtown residences.

"Suburban people tend to think they want a house next door and a neighbor that's a traditional neighbor in a house just like theirs. But downtown I feel that people don't want to pull into a cornfield and live in a house that looks just like everyone else's house. So they embrace the texture and diversity of downtown. Downtown is just about as diverse as you get in Indianapolis, but it's still not a really diverse group. We're very suburban in an urban setting. It's great—it's very comfortable."

Chatham-Arch

Like Lockerbie Square, the Chatham-Arch neighborhood (see maps **M-2** and **M-6**) also has stood at the brink of collapse in recent years.

"We had the Salvation Army band playing on the corner of 9th and Broadway at 4:30 every Sunday afternoon," recalls Susan Williams, a resident since 1981 and former member of the City-County Council. "The majority of the neighborhood was rooming houses and it was very transient and alcohol dependent."

But Chatham-Arch sobered up and recovered the integrity of a neighborhood that's long been considered significant both historically and architecturally. Says the Indianapolis Historic Preservation Commission:

"The northern portion of Chatham-Arch (map **M-2**) illustrates an unusual mixture of housing types. Here, workers' cottages, middle class residences, rental duplexes, apartment buildings and flats, commercial buildings with second-floor sleeping rooms, and a few large homes of the wealthy all existed at the turn of the century." Though the rent-out sleeping rooms are gone, many of the historic buildings remain in place.

Williams was a member of the planning group that secured the historic district designation for Chatham-Arch. She and her husband, David Rimstidt, also were among the many who invested sweat equity in restoring their homes—with plenty of friendly neighbor participation.

Williams recalls with pleasure: "So we're in there scraping wallpaper and somebody sticks their head in the window and has an opinion. Then when we were deciding what paint color we wanted on the outside we'd slop a little up and stand back and look, and people would drive by and offer an opinion. It looked like a quilt before it was done—and I ended up with boring beige." Redoing the Williams-Rimstidt house was a 20-year project that ended a few years ago, but you can still see homeowners at work on their places throughout Chatham-Arch, as well as new construction.

Who lives in Chatham-Arch? Williams thinks of her neighbors up and down the street and around the block. "A plethora of lawyers...the artistic director of the IRT [Indiana Repertory Theater] ...media folks...the Lieutenant Governor...the head of the firefighters' union...an engineer or two...empty-nester types...young families," she says. It's a pretty good mix of occupations and ages, and there's some racial diversity, though Williams would like to see more. Fifteen-twenty years ago when Chatham-Arch residents were pulling the neighborhood back up to par Williams would tell her African-American friends, "Why don't you come downtown? You can get a heck of a house for not very much money." And the response she often got was, "My family worked hard to get out of neighborhoods like that. We want to live by the golf courses."

"I think that attitude is changing," Williams says. "I think as we see the area become more complete and feel more comfortable and give a feeling of success, I think we're going to see that change. It's becoming more diverse as it becomes more comfortable."

Massachusetts Avenue is the commercial backbone of Chatham-Arch. Restaurants, theaters, art galleries, and specialty retail services along the Avenue serve both the immediate neighborhood as well as visitors from throughout the Indianapolis metropolitan area, meaning lots of traffic on nights and weekends.

St. Joseph

St. Joseph was named in 1854 by a missionary from Notre Dame University who dreamed of building a Catholic university

■ ■ ■ ■ ■ ■ ■ ■ ■ ■ ■ ■ ■ ■ ■ ■ ■ ■
Susan Williams:
"I *want to talk about the raising kids part*"

Susan Williams, CEO of the Indiana State Office Building Commission and former longtime member of the City-County Council, reared a family in the Chatham-Arch neighborhood and sent her kids to IPS schools.

"I want to talk about the raising kids part. My kids were both born in the '80s, and everybody said, well you're going to have to move out of the city. And I said, I'm going to try to get this [school decision] figured out. The fact is, Indianapolis Public Schools have extraordinary magnet programs, and my children both went to the Key School. They were there from pre-school through eighth grade. The Center for Inquiry at New Jersey Street and St. Clair—it's a fabulous school. The high school programs have a ways to go, but the math-science magnet at [Arsenal] Tech I would put up against any program in the country… And I want to tell you what we did for enrichment, too. We didn't go to the Children's Museum once a year or on a day off from school. We went probably every week. Same with the Zoo. There's a sports program at IUPUI that's incredible. Their summer programs for young kids are just remarkable. So I didn't need a country club. There was absolutely no lack of things to do within very close proximity. I was a working mom, and I could get all of that done."

▪▪▪▪▪▪▪▪▪▪▪▪▪▪▪

Bill Gray:
"Let's talk the language of affordable housing"

Bill Gray is executive director of the Riley Area Development Corporation, a nonprofit agency whose mission includes developing quality affordable housing for low to moderate income residents in downtown Indy.

"Let's talk the language of affordable housing…When we say we are in the affordable housing business that means we sell a home to somebody who earns no more than 80% of median income, and we sell them a home they can afford. The median income in Marion County is $44,850 for one person and $64,000 for a family of four…We think $116,000 is about as high a price we can sell a house to somebody who makes 80% of median income. We try to sell our houses lower than that…We either buy vacant land and build new homes or we buy an older home and rehab it… We like to buy the house as cheaply as possible and rehab it totally up to code as inspected by the city. And we sell that house at just a slight value more than what we put into it but below the assessed value so that the owner can immediately get some equity in their home…Some of the houses we've sold to young families who four years ago met the criteria of 80% but now make 110% of median income. It's not a program that punishes people—you don't have to stay at 80%. They're firemen, they're policemen, they're people who work for the state of Indiana. They're just families."

in Indianapolis and bought the future campus site for $6,000. The university never materialized but a diverse neighborhood certainly did. St. Joseph contains good examples of residential architecture spanning virtually the entire period since the 1860s. The Indianapolis Historic Preservation Commission lists these styles: Italianate, Queen Anne, Romanesque Revival, Tudor Revival, Nineteenth Century Commercial, Renaissance Revival, and Carpenter-builder—plus "the most significant collection of rowhouse buildings in the city."

St. Joseph's present-day mix of residential, commercial, and indus-trial buildings is a rich blend of land uses. Or, as Leah Orr declares, "The St. Joseph Historic Neighborhood has it all—because of the way it was designed from the beginning." Orr, a sculptor whose studio at the corner of Alabama and St. Joseph streets is a neighborhood landmark, is a community activist who has played a major role in preserving the archi-tectural integrity of St. Joseph and adjacent downtown neighborhoods, and a tireless advocate of decent, affordable housing.

When you look at St. Joseph, think of Alabama Street as the "Main Street" of this downtown neighborhood (see maps **M-3** and **M-4**). To gain a quick sense of the variety of housing in St. Joseph, note in particular:

◎ The rowhouses on the west side of Alabama Street between the Christian Place apartments (at 830 Alabama St.) and Pearson Terrace (northwest corner of Alabama and St. Joseph streets)

◎ Renaissance Tower, at 230 9th Street, a classy old apartment hotel that's popular with, among other people, professional actors in town for shows at Indiana Repertory Theatre and Murat Theatre. Downtown residents also lodge their out-of-town guests at Renaissance.

◎ The new townhouses (circa 2004) on the north side of St. Joseph Street between Hudson and Alabama.

St. Joseph is home to renters, owners, young, old, families, couples, singles, straights, gays—the kind of blend you expect to find in a downtown neighborhood. You can get a good sense of the neighborhood by spending some time at Corner Coffee, a recently established gathering place at the southwest corner of Alabama and 11th streets. Bring your laptop—the place is wired for free Internet access.

Ransom Place

Ransom Place (see map **M-16**) is the smallest of the historic downtown neighborhoods but one with particular significance for the African-American community. This is how the Indianapolis Historic Preservation Commission describes the neighborhood:

"Ransom Place developed as a small pocket of modest vernacular houses just north and west of the Mile Square and represents an early, intact neighborhood associated with the city's prominent and well-established African-American community. Today, due to the industrial and commercial expansion of the city, the three-block area remains as a reminder of an area once considered a prestigious address by the black community."

The IHPC narrative continues: "The houses of Ransom Place are primarily frame, one-story dwellings of modest vernacular styles typical of the late 19th and early 20th centuries. While many buildings have undergone alterations, they still retain their original plan and frequently their original trim and decoration. The lots are narrow, on grid-patterned streets, oriented to the diagonal Indiana Avenue, and have sidewalks and shallow setbacks."

Ransom Place is within easy walking distance of retail services along 10th Street and at Lockefield Commons; Crispus Attucks Middle School, at 1140 Dr. Martin Luther King, Jr. St.; and the cluster of university schools and major medical services establishments on the Indiana University-Purdue University Campus, immediately west and south of the neighborhood.

Wholesale District

The name "Wholesale District" makes it sound like they're pushing racks of dresses or carts of fresh fish around this downtown neighborhood. In fact, a century ago large numbers of wholesale merchants did ply their trade along South Meridian, Illinois, and Pennsylvania streets, and Maryland and Georgia (see map **M-25**). They were clustered south of Monument Circle primarily because that's where Union Station was—and still is, "America's first railroad station," according to a placard in the building. Freight depots also were nearby, making this the only sensible place for a wholesaler to set up shop. Today, some of the old loft buildings are being converted into condos and apartments, and the "Whole—" in Wholesale means a whole lot of fun and entertainment in the district. Conseco Fieldhouse, home of the Indiana Pacers, is at the southeast corner of the Wholesale District; RCA Dome, home of the Indianapolis Colts, is at the west side, on Capitol Avenue. In between are thousands of fans on game days, dozens of restaurants, an intriguing collection of bars and nightclubs, and plenty of space for people-watching, not to mention the shopping possibilities at Circle Centre mall.

The residential possibilities in the Wholesale District are still quite few—but all interesting. Presently, you can count your options on one hand:

◎ The Janus Lofts, apartments at 255 S. McCrea St., renting for $800 to $1,400 a month. The developer hints they'll be converted to condos some day. Info: 464-8254.

◎ The Harness Factory Lofts, 30 E. Georgia St., across the street from Conseco Fieldhouse. Rents range from $700 to $1,310. (See more details on this property at the discussion of apartments, later in the chapter.) Info: 632-2770.

◎ Meridian Street Lofts, 201 S. Meridian St., condos in the $229,000 to $419,000 range. Info: 290-4389.

◎ Six Over Meridian, a new condo development announced in the spring of 2004 to be built on the upper floors at 141 S. Meridian St. (over Jillian's). Announced price range: $300,000 to mid-$400,000. Info: 571-9330.

◎ The condos at 110 E. Washington St. Strictly speaking, this building stands just outside the legal boundary of the Wholesale District. But close is O.K. Info: 917-1431.

One other building simply has to be added to the list or it will be an orphan, without a neighborhood family:

◎ The Block, apartments at 50 N. Illinois St. in the historic William H. Block Department Store building. The 163 units rent for $750 to $1,200 a month (approximately $1 per square foot). Though this building is several streets north of the historic Wholesale District, it's akin in spirit. Info: 238-0100.

You can find a complete list of apartment and condominium properties in the Directory, Chapter 11.

Emerging Neighborhoods

Two downtown neighborhoods deserve special mention because of what they promise to become in the very near future. They are the Upper Canal and Market Square.

Upper Canal

This is the neighborhood on both sides of Canal Walk and generally north of North Street (see maps **M-15** and **M-19**). Sizeable apartment complexes in this neighborhood have become popular with downtown workers, IUPUI faculty and staff, and medical school and law school students, among others. (See apartment details later in this chapter.)

Some of downtown Indy's priciest new properties are in the gated community called Watermark, on the east side of Canal Walk between Walnut and North streets (**M-19**). Big new houses stand on narrow lots, city style, to encourage neighborliness, and were selling upwards of $500,000 in 2004.

The far north end of Upper Canal holds perhaps the most interesting prospects for future residential development downtown. In 2003, Clarian

Health, the hospital consortium uniting Methodist, IU, and Riley hospitals, broke ground for a laboratory north of 11th Street (**M-15**) that eventually will employ more than a thousand people. The arrival of this major new employer in the Northwest Quadrant is expected to spark new retail stores and living spaces in the immediate area. By 2020 there could be 1,400 new residences on the blocks north of St. Clair Street, according to projections by the Indianapolis Regional Center Plan 2020, adopted in 2004.

Market Square

People who've lived in or around Indy for a few years remember when the old Market Square Arena was imploded in a puff of smoke on July 8, 2001. Vacant since then, the MSA site (see map **M-24A**) is expected to begin sprouting new housing as early as 2004. Two major projects are in the works:

◎ Market Square Partners announced plans in February 2004 to build two 22-story condominium towers containing a total of 400 condos starting at $130,000 and capping around $1 million—average price, $312,000. Some units will be available for qualified low-income purchasers. Construction could begin in the fall of 2004 and the first move-ins in 2006. Plans also call for a cluster of low-rise retail stores and public spaces on the site. Market Street will be the "Main Street" of this new community.

◎ City Centre Associates, LLC, announced plans in early 2004 to build a four-story condominium called The Hudson on a present parking lot at the southwest corner of New Jersey and Ohio streets, immediately north of the proposed Market Square high-rise. Seventy-five units are planned at the City Centre site. If construction begins in summer 2004, units could be ready for occupancy by the fall of 2005, the developer says. A related company, Kosene & Kosene, already has built two large condominiums on East Ohio Street—The Clevelander and The Packard (**M-11**).

Renting an Apartment Downtown

Downtown Indy has a large inventory of apartment space—and it's hot property, apartment owners say. As the downtown scene has blossomed with new cafes, bars, entertainment venues, and recreational options, living in the thick of it all has grown increasingly popular with the young working crowd, including professionals arriving in Indy from places like Chicago and New York. In the spring of 2004, the Van Rooy Companies, largest owner-manager of rental properties downtown, reported a 96 percent occupancy rate of the buildings it owns. The following table provides a quick look at some of the apartment choices that are Van Rooy holdings but representative of the market as a whole:

Apartment Name	Address	Sizes	Rent Range
Apollo Aurora	1101 N. Alabama St.	1 BR	$575
Garden Arch	726-728 N. East St.	1 BR	$639-$650
Pennsylvania	919 N. Pennsylvania St.	1 BR & Townhomes	$850-$950
Real Silk Lofts	611 N. Park Av.	1 BR & 1 BR Lofts	$999-$1299
Turnverein	902 N. Meridian St.	Studio, 1 & 2 BR	$650-$2500
Utomin	11th St. & College Av.	1 & 2 BR	$440-$540
Vermont Place Properties:			
Continental Towers	410 N. Meridian St.	1 & 2 BR	$665-$1320
Blacherne	402 N. Meridian St.	*Under development*	
Link Savoy	401 N. Illinois St.	*Under development*	

The rent range of those properties—$440 to $2,500—represents pretty well the current downtown apartment market, and there are many other choices, including:

◎ *Riley Towers*, 650 N. Alabama St., 635-3300, **Map M-8**
   Riley, the high-rise apartment buildings on North Alabama Street, offers studios of 355-655 sq. ft. renting for $510 to $664; and penthouses measuring 1,800-2,000 sq. ft. for $2,455 to $2,905; and practically every size in between. Riley also offers furnished and corporate apartments, and short term leases ranging from 3 to 8 months.

◎ *Canal Overlook Apartments*, 430 Indiana Av., 634-6090, **Map M-19**
   Located on Canal Walk and only two blocks from the Capitol, Canal Overlook offers efficiency, studio, 1 BR, and 2 BR floor plans; sizes ranging from 456 sq. ft. to 1,023 sq. ft.; and basic rents from $640 to $990. Short-term leases and corporate suites available.

◎ *The Gardens of Canal Court,* 434 Canal Court South Dr., 636-2126, **Map M-15 & 19**

One-bedroom apartments are offered in seven sizes ranging from 875 to 1,093 sq. ft., with rents from $827 to $990. Two-bedroom apartments come in eight floor plans, sizes ranging from 1,160 to 1,311 sq. ft. Rents for these units range from $932 to $1,177. All units have gas fireplaces.

◎ *Lockefield Gardens,* 737 Lockefield Ln., 631-2922, **Map M-16**

The original brick buildings at this large modern site next to IUPUI are National Historic Landmarks—built as public housing in the 1930s and considered models of affordable housing at the time. One-bedroom units, 514 sq. ft., begin at $557 and range up to $654 for 723 sq. ft. Two-bedroom units, from $596 for 602 sq. ft. to $937 for 1,450 sq. ft.

◎ *The Harness Factory Lofts,* 30 E. Georgia St., 632-2770, **Map M-25**

This is one of the early factory-to-apartment conversions downtown, dating to 1987. And when they say "loft," they mean it: ceilings are 14 feet high; windows, 9-foot-4. Carpet covers the foot-thick concrete floors. Conseco Fieldhouse is right across the street. Rents begin at $700 for a 645 sq. ft. studio and range up to $1,310 for a 1,290 sq. ft., 2 BR 2 BA unit.

Please see the Directory for a complete list of downtown apartments.

What to look for in an apartment

Angie Overton, leasing director of Van Rooy, provides these tips to apartment hunters in downtown Indy—a few things to look for when you're looking around:

◎ A *good security plan.* Best idea is intercom control of visitor entry.

◎ *Upscale appointments.* Most renters insist on hardwood floors, Overton says. New kitchens and new baths are in demand.

◎ A *pet policy your pet can live with.* Practically all apartments accept cats. Very few accept dogs. The problem with dogs downtown is the lack of space for them to run. (Of course, all dog owners are expected to pick up what their pooches drop along the way.) Virtually all apartment owners add a monthly extra for pets. Van Rooy does so and charges a $200 nonrefundable one-time fee, as well.

◎ A *parking policy that you can live with*. The best arrangement is for parking to be included in the rent, Overton says.

◎ A *responsive maintenance department, 24 hours a day*. Nothing makes renters unhappier faster than undependable maintenance, so check out the service level in advance.

How do you get answers to all these questions? Overton suggests looking at the apartment owner's web site for details. And ask for references from present renters.

Getting a Nose for the Condos

Most of the new downtown residences currently under construction or proposed for the short-term—two or three years out—are condominiums. Everyone knows what a condo is, right?

In this book, "condo" means a large building—perhaps newly built, perhaps an old factory or office building converted into living space—containing a number of privately-owned living units. They may be one-floor units, very much like apartments; or two-floor, townhouse-style units. They can even be penthouses with gardens (Indy already has a few of those). Most condo residents share hallways and outside entrance doors with their neighbors. But a few condos downtown are completely self-contained townhouses, with their own front doors and back doors. They just happen to be built smack up against the neighboring property and share the cost of services and upkeep. So much for definitions.

You can count the currently occupied downtown condominiums on two hands:

◎ *The Avenue*, 436 Massachusetts Av.
◎ *The Clevelander*, Ohio St. between New Jersey & Cleveland Sts.
◎ *Firehouse Square*, Ohio St. between Alabama & New Jersey Sts.
◎ *The Glencoe*, 627 N. Pennsylvania St.
◎ *Indianapolis Glove Co.*, 430 N. Park Av.
◎ *Lockerbie Terrace*, 225 N. New Jersey St.
◎ *110 E. Washington St.*
◎ *The Packard*, 450 E. Ohio St.
◎ *Real Silk Lofts*, 611 N. Park Av.

Those buildings contain about 300 residences total. But if all the proposed plans for additional condos come to fruition, 375-400 more condos could be on the market by 2006. These projects were proposed or underway as of mid-2004:

- ◎ *Chatham Point,* College St. & Massachusetts Av., 27 units
- ◎ *Conrad Hotel,* Illinois & Washington Sts., 18 units
- ◎ *The Hudson,* Ohio & New Jersey Sts., 75 units
- ◎ *Indianapolis Athletic Club,* 350 N. Meridian St., 44 units
- ◎ *Meridian Street Lofts,* 201 S. Meridian St., 18 units
- ◎ *Mill No. 9,* College & Walnut Sts., 44 units
- ◎ *The Residences at Market Square,* Market & New Jersey Sts., 200 units (in the first of two planned high-rise buildings)
- ◎ *Six Over Meridian,* 141 S. Meridian St., 21 units

Best way to scout the condo scene is to pick a fine day, put on your walking shoes, and use the maps in the back of this book as your guide to a little stroll around the downtown condo territory. That will show you exactly what's happening. Every project that's up and running should have price info in full view. But just as a reference point, the 71 condominiums sold in downtown Indy during 2003 averaged $202,455, according to the Metropolitan Indianapolis Board of Realtors (MIBOR).

Shopping for a Regular House

Regular in this sense means "detached, single-family dwelling," in other words a suburban-style house. Not a townhouse, rowhouse, condo, or apartment. A regular house. If that's what you're looking for, downtown Indy offers many possibilities, and most of the market is in the Northeast Quadrant neighborhoods: Lockerbie Square, Chatham-Arch, St. Joseph. Fletcher Place also offers a number of possibilities and Ransom Place a few.

Your best strategy is to drive around and see what's being offered for sale, do some searching on the Internet, and enlist the help of a real estate professional who specializes in downtown residential properties. A few of the better known downtown specialists are Joe Everhart, Sycamore Group, 916-1052; Kurt Flock, Flock Realty, 634-6676; and Joan Lonneman, F.C. Tucker, 259-8600.

Cost trends? According to MIBOR, the 45 single-family downtown homes that sold during 2001 averaged $207,638; the 39 sold during 2002 averaged $269,176; and the 45 sold during 2003 averaged $255,536. To give you just a bit of an idea of what's available currently, following are a few houses that were listed in the spring of 2004 on the website www.MIBOR.org:

- ◎ 1013 N. Alabama St., 1890 Federal style, 2,347 sq. ft., 3 BR, 3 BA, 2-car detached garage, $210,000.
- ◎ 640 E. New York St., 1902 Victorian, 2,405 sq. ft., 3 BR, 2 BA, assigned parking, $229,900.
- ◎ 833 Wright St., 1939 bungalow, 925 sq. ft., 2 BR, 2 BA, no garage, $129,900.
- ◎ 605 E. McCarty St., 1890 bungalow, 1,920 sq. ft., 2 BR, 2 BA, 1-car detached garage, $145,900.
- ◎ 617 Fletcher Av., 1900 historic style, 2,514 sq. ft., 3 BR, 3 BA, 2-car detached garage, $199,900.
- ◎ 738 Elm St., 1900 Victorian, 2,000 sq. ft., 3 BR, 2 BA, 2-car detached garage, $269,900.
- ◎ 338+ N. College Av., 1900 Federal style, 3,574 sq. ft., 4 BR, 2 BA, no garage, $224,000.
- ◎ 322 N. East St., 1984 townhouse, 2,160 sq. ft., 3 BR, 3 BA, 2-car detached garage, $289,500.

Moving In and Hooking Up

This chapter is about—*taking possession*. Don't you just love those words? Possession! Like Columbus, you're planting your flag on space that's never before borne your good name. You're claiming the territory, creating a new residence that is uniquely *you*, a brand new gathering place for your network of friends, colleagues, and—who knows—interesting new acquaintances. So start planning a party!

But first—there's the matter of relocating your worldly goods from there to here, and getting the lights turned on. If you're leasing an apartment downtown, the moving-in part probably will follow simple guidelines from the building manager, like no move-ins at midnight. Generally, apartment managers try to make it easy. Some even offer the free use of a moving van within a 50-mile radius. Your biggest challenge may be scheduling your move date for a time that takes maximum advantage of free help (including those willing volunteers who have promised to help you move the hide-a-bed and 42-inch TV) and minimizes traffic jams.

Hint: Apartment leasing directors in Indy say the busiest move-in month is May. August is close behind. If your schedule calls for a May or August move, better make plans early to reserve whatever equipment and labor you'll need. And if your window of opportunity is June or July—well, that can be crunch time, too, so plan ahead.

Another hint: If you can schedule your move for one of the slower months on the apartment leasing scene—November, December, January, February—you may not only avoid the hassles of the spring-summer months but also have a wider choice of available units.

Hooking up the utilities—electricity, gas, telephone, cable—is fairly easy in most apartments and requires little more than a few phone calls to switch accounts to your name. Apartment managers can provide the phone numbers. This chapter also contains a reference list for you.

If your new residence downtown is a condominium, townhouse, or detached single-family dwelling, you may need a few more details concerning the utilities. Again, full particulars lie ahead for:

- The electric company—IPL
- The gas company—Citizens Gas
- The water company—Indianapolis Water
- The cable TV company—Bright House Networks

The chapter also contains reference information for the principal telephone company serving downtown—the company that actually owns the telephone wires:

- SBC

Of course, you do have other choices for telephone and TV program service aside from the hard-wired, conventional route; in fact, so many choices that it's impossible to account for them all in any useful way in this book. But check out the chapter section on Wi-Fi in downtown Indy. The hot spots downtown can give you an Internet connection while you're deciding on more permanent arrangements.

Indianapolis Power & Light Co.–IPL

www.ipalco.com

2102 N. Illinois St., Indianapolis

To pay bills: P.O. Box 110, Indianapolis, IN 46206-0110

317-261-8222 or toll-free 888-261-8222.

Customer service hours: Mon-Fri, 7 a.m. to 8 p.m.; Sat, 8 a.m. to 12 Noon

Online account services.

The web address above will lead you to the main menu of services where you can connect, transfer, or terminate services. At the home page, click on "Your Home," then on "Connect or Transfer Service Online." You can also pay your bill online.

Rates.

Information at the company website for Rate RS, Residential Service, specifies a basic monthly charge ("Customer Charge") and an additional charge for electricity consumed ("Energy Charge"). As you will see in these details, the lowest rate over 1,000 kilowatt hours per month is for residences that use electric heat or electric water heating, or both. Many new condos downtown are all-electric.

Customer Charge:

    For bills of 0-325 KWH/month $6.70/month

    For bills over 325 KWH/month $11.00/month

Energy Charge:

    Any part of the first 500 KWH/month. . . . . 6.70¢/KWH

    Over 500 KWH/month. . . . . 4.40¢/KWH

With electric heating and/or water heating

    Over 1,000 KWH/month . . . . 3.18¢/KWH

IPL offers some of the lowest residential electricity rates in the nation. A table at the company web site presents these comparison costs for 1,000 kilowatt hours per month for general residential service, as of 7/1/2001:

Indianapolis $66.76

Denver 68.75

Charlotte 79.06

Milwaukee 82.91

Washington, DC	93.56
Baltimore	95.31
Dallas	101.23
Chicago	101.80
Houston	110.41
Philadelphia	142.70
San Francisco	156.92
Boston	163.04
New York City	197.46

Citizens Gas

www.citizensgas.com
2020 N. Meridian St., Indianapolis
317-924-3311 or toll-free 800-GAS-4217
Customer service hours: Mon-Fri, 7 a.m. to 8 p.m.; Sat, 7:30 a.m. to 4:30 p.m.

Online account services.

At the home page, click on "Residential" (upper left). That will lead you to the full menu of services including new connections and bill paying. Notice there's an Español option, too. You can also call one of the telephone numbers above.

Rates.

As of June 1, 2003, Gas Rate No. D1, covering residential domestic service, calls for a basic monthly charge of $6.65 plus 17.7 cents per therm.

S-s-s-s-steam heat, anyone?

If you are of a certain vintage you may have grown up listening to the soothing winter hiss of steam in the home radiators. If you long to recapture that warmth of yesteryear (and have buckets of money to spend on nostalgia), be advised that Citizens Gas also distributes steam throughout the downtown area. Virtually all the customers are commercial and high-rise buildings. But if your dwelling place is on one of the streets where the steam lines run, you might look into this option. Steam heat is expensive, however. A posting at the Citizens Gas website details a $32 per month minimum charge plus $1.16 per therm for the first 1,000 therms. Compare that to $6.65 monthly plus 17.7¢ per therm for natural gas.

Indianapolis Water

www.indianapoliswater.com

1220 Waterway Blvd., Indianapolis

Mailing address: P.O. Box 1220, Indianapolis, IN 46206

317-631-1431 or toll-free 877-631-1431

Customer service hours: Mon-Fri, 7 a.m. to 7 p.m.; Sat, 8 a.m. to noon

Online account services.

Indianapolis Water provides an attractive and easy to use website with some nifty added features. Besides making arrangements for water service and paying your bill online, you can:

- ◎ View the current reservoir level (to make sure we're not running out of water) and
- ◎ Check all the weather activity throughout the Midwest and the U.S. as a whole. Click on the button labeled "View Current Local Weather" and you'll go straight to the National Weather Service. Many, many viewing choices there including "looping" radar maps that show the movement of weather fronts for the past hour or so.

Rates.

A posting at the company website indicates a monthly base charge of $7.55 for a ⅝-inch water pipe and $9.10 for a ¾-inch pipe (common sizes for residential service); and consumption rates of $1.29 per 100 cubic feet for the first 1,500 cubic feet (11,250 gallons).

Leah Orr:

How to "Own" Your Place Downtown

Sculptor Leah Orr has been a leader in the St. Joseph neighborhood for more than 20 years—and a strong influence on the success of other downtown projects, including the Davlan Apartments on Massachusetts Avenue. She serves on the board of the Riley Area Development Corporation.

"It's good to have people want to move into my neighborhood. But I'm disappointed by some of the newcomers. Number one they don't seem to want to come out of their houses and get known. Number two they don't want to participate in neighborhood matters. Number three they're less culturally and racially diversified. If you're going to quote-unquote 'protect your investment' moneywise you have to participate. If you're going to keep the neighborhood safe you must know your neighbors. You must be a nosy neighbor. People think because they own a house they have control. But the only ownership you have is what you give back to the ongoing development of the community."

Bright House Networks—Cable Service

www.indy.rr.com

3030 Roosevelt Av., Indianapolis (I-70 at Keystone/Rural exit)

317-972-9700

Customer service hours: Mon-Thurs, 7:30 a.m. to 6:30; Fri, 7:30 a.m. to 7 p.m.; Sat, 8:30 a.m. to 4 p.m. Call center staffed 7 a.m. to 11 p.m. every day.

Rates.

From the company website, following is a very abbreviated list of services and monthly rates effective January 2004. Go to the website or call Bright House for full details:

Basic Cable Service	$11.85
Standard Service (available only with Basic)	$29.20
Full Cable Service	$41.05
Digital Access Tier	$ 4.95
Digital Receiver	$ 6.55
New Installation	$49.64
Apartment Installation	$16.55
HBO (14 screens)	$10.00

SBC

www.sbc.com

220 N. Meridian St., Indianapolis

800-742-8771

Customer service hours: Mon-Fri, 7 a.m. to 7 p.m.; Sat, 8 a.m. to 5 p.m.

Online account services.

At the SBC Home page, click on "Residential Customers." That will bring up a whole range of service options including new phone service, Internet on SBC Yahoo! DSL or Dial, wireless Internet, and digital satellite TV. Of course, you can also do all these things by calling the 800 number listed above. The online option lets you look at your bill—and pay it, too.

Repair service.

Dial 800-868-9696. The hours of operation are Mon-Fri, 7 a.m. to 10 p.m.; Sat-Sun, 7 a.m. to 9 p.m.

For Empty-Nesters Only

So you're rattling around in a great big house that you love to death but it's really more than you need with the kids gone and you're thinking wouldn't it be nice to have less to take care of in the way of real estate—not to mention all those gas and electric bills that just about broke the bank last year.

Does any of that sound familiar? If so, you may be ready to move to a condo in downtown Indy. Empty-nesters, former suburbanites, are a growing presence on the downtown scene. One of the attractions of condo life is the money you can save on utility bills compared to living in a conventional single-family house. To illustrate what's possible, the numbers below show what the author and his mate experienced when they moved from a charming, 1910-vintage, 2,700-square-foot house in the suburbs to a 2002-vintage, 1,700-square-foot condo within four blocks of Monument Circle:

January 2002		January 2004	
Still Heating the Big House in the 'Burbs		**Home Sweet Home in the Downtown Condo**	
Electricity	$98.97	Electricity	$71.30
Natural gas	189.72	Natural gas	10.18
Water, sewer, garbage	89.08	Water, sewer, garbage	15.85
TOTAL	$377.77	TOTAL	$97.33

Some footnotes to those numbers: Concerning costs of the big old family house, we heated it with an ancient gas furnace that had been converted many years before from coal. But the house was well insulated and fitted with tight, double-pane windows. Also, the suburban city had recently built a new sewage treatment plant, and utility customers were paying off the bonds that financed that municipal improvement. The garbage-recycling portion of the bill was about $14 a month.

The new condo is a two-floor unit with windows on the north and south. It's in the center of the building, so there are other units (heated spaces) on both sides as well as below—lots of protection from winter cold and summer heat. The place is all-electric, and all the juice comes from IPL, which sells electricity at one of the lowest rates in the nation. The only time we use natural gas is when we flick on the cute little fake fireplace. The south-facing windows are covered with reflective film to reduce glare and heat. We keep the thermostat at 73 degrees winter and summer.

The whole equation of moving from a conventional suburban house into a new condo downtown includes many factors—taxes, maintenance, and the like. But we're really happy to cut our January electric-gas bill by $200—more money for fun! Besides, consuming less energy is a good thing.

Going Online Free with Wi-Fi

If you're the outgoing sort—downtowners are by definition—note these several locations where connecting to the Internet is free. All you bring to the deal is your laptop computer rigged for Wireless Fidelity, or Wi-Fi. In the hotels listed, the lobby area is the hot spot.

- *The Abbey*, coffeehouse at 771 Massachusetts Av. (corner of College Av.)
- *Adam's Mark Hotel*, 120 W. Market St.
- *Canterbury Hotel*, 123 S. Illinois St.
- *Corner Coffee*, 251 E. 11th St. (corner of Alabama St.)
- *Hilton Garden Inn*, 10 E. Market St.
- *Monument Circle*, The entire outdoor area, compliments of the Columbia Club
- *Starbucks Coffee*, 430 Massachusetts Av.
  Presently this is a free plug-in operation, but staff say that all company stores are due to become wireless.

CHAPTER 3

Going Shopping

First the good news. Downtown Indy has some great stores that attract shoppers from a wide area. The big concentration is at Circle Centre Mall, home to dozens of specialty stores, two big department stores—Nordstrom and Parisian—plus all those tempting eating establishments where you can recharge your batteries after a strenuous round of retailing. The back of this chapter contains a full list of the Circle Centre establishments. And if you'd rather drive there than walk from your downtown abode, you can park below Circle Centre for the incredibly low rate of $1 for 3 hours or less. That's almost as cheap as living above the store.

Downtown Indy also has art galleries, delis, a farmers' market, a leather supply store, an upholstery fabric store, a tobacconist—even a pipe organ builder if that's what you need for your place. All of the special retail niches downtown are listed in the Directory at the back of the book.

Finding the Furniture Store

Now for the not-so-good news. When it comes to the everyday necessities of life, especially life when you're settling into a new downtown residence, downtown Indy can test your patience. You may be surprised to know that downtown does *not* have as of mid-2004:

- ◎ A home improvements store. No Home Depot. No Menard's. No Lowe's. (But you can buy some of the basics downtown—studs, Sheetrock, hardware—check the Directory. The arrival of True Value in mid-2004, at Lockerbie Marketplace (**M-11**), was a cause of some celebration. But for big-box home improvements, you've got to drive back toward the suburbs.)
- ◎ A first-class supermarket. No big Marsh. No big Kroger.
- ◎ A furniture store. No Kittle's, La-Z-Boy, or BedroomOne.
- ◎ A routine discount store. No Target or Meijer. Wal-Mart has made no overtures.
- ◎ A computer or electronics store. No Radio Shack or CompUSA.

That's only a partial list. As a downtown resident you quickly adjust to this curious void of certain kinds of stores, planning your trips to the outlying malls the way folks used to hitch up for a trot out to Grandma's house. Over the river, through the woods, and all that. But it's true: Downtown is set up for fine shopping, impulse buying, and psyche-soothing indulgence, but not for much of the routine shopping associated with settling and maintaining a residence.

Groceries.

You can buy groceries downtown but your choices are limited to two stores. One is O'Malia's, an institution downtown and the anchor store of Lockerbie Marketplace (**M-11**). O'Malia's is more than a grocery store; it's a meeting place. Shop there regularly and you'll experience the rich variety of people who live downtown—young and old, coifed and unkempt, black and white, gay and straight, rich and poor, professional and day laborer, homeless and landed gentry. And even though shelf space is limited in this former Sears, Roebuck building, you'll find just about everything on your shopping list. Marsh Supermarkets, owner of the O'Malia stores, is planning improvements to the downtown store.

To supplement their grocery shopping some downtowners make regular runs to the Marsh at 82nd and Allisonville Rd., with a side-stop at Trader Joe's, a couple of blocks east on 82nd; and a swing by Wild Oats, at 1300 E. 86th St.

The other grocery store downtown is Sav-A-Lot, on 10th Street in the Northwest Quadrant (**M-16**), where the sign on the door says it all: "No fancy shelving, limited varieties, no kumquats."

Attracting More Stores—Reaching "Critical Mass"

When downtowners ask why they have to drive to Castleton, Greenwood, or Avon for ordinary, everyday shopping, the answer experts give is "critical mass," meaning population. Downtown doesn't have enough resident population yet to attract interest from certain kinds of stores, the ones that rely on regular, repeat visits from a large, nearby group of residents.

So, what is the population of downtown? The 2000 Census counted about 12,000 people. Today? A number you hear often is 17,000—cited recently, for example, by real estate firm Colliers, Turley, Martin, Tucker. But population numbers are tricky. The Census Bureau tally includes people residing in jails, for example. So the 2000 figures for downtown include citizens temporarily at home in the Marion County lockup. The Census also counts students living on campus, like residents in IUPUI housing for undergraduates and graduate students. Jailbirds don't go shopping; students do. Numberwise, it's probably a wash.

What are the expectations about future downtown population? The Indianapolis Regional Center Plan 2020, adopted in the spring of 2004, makes a priority of reaching 40,000 downtown residents by 2020. Note

Stretching your dollar

Grocery shopping downtown may need improving, but the cost of groceries in Indy generally is lower than the rest of the nation. According to info posted by the Indianapolis Chamber of Commerce at its website (indychamber.com), groceries here cost 93.2% of the U.S. average (100.0) based on a study conducted during the second quarter of 2002. Overall cost of living in Indianapolis also is very favorable compared to other cities. Combining the cost of groceries, housing, utilities, transportation, health care, and miscellaneous goods and services, the study cited above pegs Indianapolis at 93.4. By comparison: St. Louis, 102.6; Cleveland, 103.9; Washington, D.C., 123.7; Chicago, 149.8; New York City (Manhattan), 220.1.

that's a "priority," not a forecast; and also note that the Regional Center extends a bit beyond downtown as defined in this book, reaching north to 16th Street and west, past the White River, to railroad tracks running on a northwesterly line from Harding Street.

At what point will the headcount be large enough to attract serious attention of the retailers that downtown residents need? Hard to say. Some people believe the number has to be in the mid-20,000 range. One of the most hopeful developments is the new plan for high-rise condos on the old Market Square Arena site. Preliminary drawings show space for retail stores on the site, presumably aimed at the daily shopping needs of the 200 to 400 new residences that may materialize there. The birth of the new Market Square community also could help to diversify retail choices across Alabama Street at the Indianapolis City Market, a popular weekday luncheon spot but skewed too much toward short orders and deli grub.

Shopping at Circle Centre:
A Directory of Stores & Services

All phone numbers are 317 area.

Accessories
Claire's Accessories 423-9072
Coach 637-2510
Hat World 972-0694
In Stitches 951-9335
Sunglass Hut 634-8535

Cards/Books/Gifts/Stationery
American Greetings 974-0924
Brookstone 624-9117
Doubleday Book Shop 632-4910
Successories 916-9643
The Children's Museum Store 634-3974
Things Remembered 638-0168

Children's Fashions

Gap Kids 631-0100
Gymboree 635-2443
The Children's Place 917-1483
The Disney Store 261-1608
The Limited Too 632-4119

Department Stores

Nordstrom 636-2121
Parisian 971-6310

Entertainment

Brewski's Sport & Wing Shack 630-5483
EBX 423-3362
Flashbaxx 630-5483
Gameworks Studio 226-9267
Gator's 630-5483
Sam Goody 267-9767
United Artists Theatre 237-6356

Health & Beauty

Bath & Body Works 632-0639
GNC/Live Well 955-9145
gym 2.0 951-1475
Origins 955-1385
Trade Secret 423-0222

Home Furnishings

Brookstone 624-9117
The White Barn Candle Company 632-3229
Yankee Candle 951-8510

Jewelry

Claire's Accessories 423-9072
Dakota Watch Company 624-9115
Feel the Bead 965-5831

J. Sterling 955-0719

Nominations. 636-7700

Nordstrom Fine Jewelry 636-2121

Parisian Fine Jewelry 971-6310

Piercing Pagoda 917-0840

Reflection Jewelers. 637-3193

Silverado. 624-9116

Watch Station 681-8725

Men's Fashions

Abercrombie & Fitch 756-8121

Aéropostale 631-1725

American Eagle Outfitters 917-9536

Banana Republic 631-0400

Eddie Bauer 632-4441

Express Men. 261-0950

Gap 631-0100

Hollister Co. 917-1006

Man Alive 916-5799

PacSun 951-0048

Music/Electronics/Video

EBX. 423-3362

Sam Goody. 267-9767

The Children's Museum Store 634-3974

Restaurants (order at the counter)

Asian Chao 488-0082

Café Nordstrom 636-2121

Cajun & Grill. 630-4541

Chick-fil-A. 822-8501

Frullati Café 634-4847

Le Petit Bistro. 634-4209

Maki of Japan 917-8908

Nick's Gyros and Yogurt 236-1969

Sbarro 638-5811
Steak Escape 236-1909
Subway 634-8263

Restaurants (order via wait staff)

Alcatraz Brewing Company 488-1230
Bertolini's Authentic Trattoria 638-1800
Brewski's Sport & Wing Shack 630-5483
Champps Restaurant 951-0033
Johnny Rockets 238-0444
Nordstrom Grill 636-2121
P.F. Chang's China Bistro 974-5747
Palomino 974-0400
Ruth's Chris Steak House 633-1313

Services

AT&T Wireless 630-4928
Cingular Wireless 681-0524
gym 2.0 951-1475
Simon Marketplace 681-8000
T-Mobile 637-0254
Trade Secret 423-0222
Verizon Wireless 964-0294
Wireless Dimensions 423-3057

Shoes

Aldo Shoes 638-0635
Ann Taylor 638-5330
Clarks England/Bostonian 635-8722
Finish Line 634-7553
Johnston & Murphy 226-9464
Man Alive 916-5799
Nine West 635-6719
Nordstrom 636-2121
Parisian 971-6310

Specialty Food

Auntie Anne's Pretzels 639-5104

Ben & Jerry's Ice Cream Shop 637-2820

Café Nordstrom 636-2121

Cinnabon 261-1258

Einstein Brothers Bagels 917-9888

Godiva Chocolatier 630-1740

Great American Cookie Co 636-3632

Maggie Moo's Ice Cream 423-3504

Nick's Café 917-9990

Nordstrom Espresso Bar 636-2121

Sweet Factory 633-4909

Specialty Shops

Bag 'n Baggage 269-0223

Brickyard Authentics 955-1500

Brookstone 624-9117

Colts Pro Shop 639-2857

Dakota Watch Company 624-9115

Field of Dreams 636-8229

Franklin Covey 917-2073

Gillani Perfumes 916-5732

Hat World 972-0694

Pacers Home Court II 262-9962

Successories 916-9643

The Children's Museum Store 634-3974

The Disney Store 261-1608

The White Barn Candle Company 632-3229

Thunder Alley Racing 638-7223

Yankee Candle 951-8510

Toys & Games

FAO Schwarz Fifth Avenue (Parisian) 971-6310

The Children's Museum Store 634-3974

Women's Fashions

Abercrombie & Fitch	756-8121
Aéropostale	631-1725
American Eagle Outfitters	917-9536
Ann Taylor	638-5330
Banana Republic	631-0400
Eddie Bauer	632-4441
Express	767-1647
Forever 21	633-2100
Gap	631-0100
Hollister Co.	917-1006
Lane Bryant	756-7503
Lerner New York	262-8757
Man Alive	916-5799
PacSun	951-0048
Talbots	636-6044
Victoria's Secret	267-9452
Wet Seal	951-0955

CHAPTER 4

Eating Out

Downtown Indy has plenty of great places to eat—you won't go hungry. But if you're a newcomer to downtown you'll need some time to develop your personal list of favorite spots, restaurants where you've dined often enough that you know the menu reflects your tastes, the service is dependable, and the value-price equation works out right.

To get up to speed on the downtown eating scene, make it a habit to pick up the publications that regularly review restaurants:

- ◎ IN*take*
- ◎ *Lockerbie Letter*
- ◎ NUVO
- ◎ *Up Down Town*

Free copies of these tabloid newspapers are available at many locations downtown. The other regular sources of restaurant reviews are:

- ◎ *Indianapolis Monthly* magazine, available at newsstands, by subscription, or at the Indianapolis-Marion County Public Library (see Directory for location).
- ◎ *Weekend* section of the *Indianapolis Star*, on Fridays.

You can also ask friends and acquaintances for their personal restaurant reviews. But remember to sprinkle those opinions with a grain of salt—or a shot of A-1. People disagree about restaurants. You say the food is swill, I say it's swell. I say the service is awful, you say you're treated like royalty. I say it's pricey but worth it, you say the place is ridiculously expensive.

When you consider the number of variables that share the table with you every time you eat out, it's no wonder that opinions on restaurants can differ so widely. Your mood, your health, your companions at table, your wallet (or expense account), the occasion, the weather, your server's personal life, the chef's headache, the food you loved as a kid—they all influence your opinion of every experience eating out.

For those reasons this chapter steers clear of restaurant ratings. I know, I know—that's cowardly. But you really do have to scout the restaurant scene on your own, and given your solemn promises concerning waistline and cholesterol, that will take you awhile. It's taken the author and spouse two years just to start getting familiar with downtown dining options. We have a short list of *our* favorite spots, which we humbly present at the end of the chapter. That doesn't mean there won't be other places on our personal list in time.

As you begin to compile your own list of favorite restaurants, this chapter can help. The "Alpha" list presented here shows all the establishments including hours and price range. The "Cuisine" list is self-explanatory. The "Eating Local" list is political—and why not? Is there any place more political than downtown Indy, especially when the Legislature is in session? So, here's the lineup, for your reference:

◎ The list of downtown Indy restaurants that are locally owned.
◎ The list of restaurants by cuisine or specialty.
◎ The complete list of establishments alphabetically, including hours and price range.

Note: Restaurant listings in this chapter are limited to table-service establishments that are open in the evening, though they may also serve lunch. The complete list of downtown restaurants appears in the Directory, at the back of the book.

Eating Local

Restaurant ownership—local versus non-local—is a big deal in downtown Indy. (For this purpose, non-local means the owner also operates restaurants in other states.) All of us are proud of local ownership and do our best to support local restaurateurs; we have some very good locally owned establishments. We are also thankful for the added choices and high-quality dining that non-local restaurant owners bring to downtown Indy. But we are aware that non-local ownership is heavier here than in the rest of the country: Experts say the customary mix is 60% locally owned, 40% non-locally owned, but in Indy the numbers are reversed. So, pay attention to ownership.

Downtown Restaurants—The Locally-owned Group

Acapulco Joe's Mexican Foods

Aesop's Tables

Agio

Amici's Downtown Italian Restaurant

Bazbeaux Pizza

Bistro Tchopstix

Bourbon Street Distillery

The Bosphorus

City Café

Cozy Restaurant & Cocktail Lounge

Downtown Olly's Restaurant/
   Sports Bar

Dunaway's

The Elbow Room Pub & Deli

Elements

El Sol de Tala Mexican
   Restaurante y Cantina

English Ivy's

Greek Islands Restaurant

Hoaglin To Go Café Marketplace

Iaria's Italian Restaurant

Jaguar Restaurant & Bar

The Living Room Lounge

Lockerbie Pub

Loughmiller's Pub & Eatery

MacNiven's Scottish-American
   Restaurant & Bar

Malibu on Maryland

Metro

Mikado Japanese

Milano Inn

Old Point Tavern

Ralph's Great Divide

Rathskeller Restaurant

R Bistro

Red Eye Café

Restaurant at the Canterbury

St. Elmo Steak House

Scholars Inn Gourmet Café & Wine Bar

745 Bar & Grill

Slippery Noodle Inn

Yats

Downtown Restaurants By Cuisine

American
Bourbon Street Distillery
Chammps Americana
Circle City Bar & Grille
The Eagle's Nest Restaurant
The Elbow Room Pub & Deli
Hard Rock Café
Hard Times Café
Malibu on Maryland
Nordstrom Grill
Old Point Tavern
Palomino Restaurant Rotisseria Bar
Payton's Place
Ralph's Great Divide
Rock Bottom Restaurant & Brewery
Scholars Inn Gourmet Café & Wine Bar
Slippery Noodle Inn

American Innovative
Elements
R Bistro

Asian
Bistro Tchopstix
India Garden Restaurant
Mikado Japanese Restaurant &
   Sushi Bar
P.F. Chang's China Bistro

Cajun
Yats

European/Continental
Aesop's Tables
The Restaurant at the Canterbury

German
The Rathskeller Restaurant

Greek
Greek Islands Restaurant

Irish
The Claddagh Irish Pub

Italian
Agio
Amici's Downtown Italian Restaurant
Bertolini's Authentic Trattoria
Buca di Beppo
Dunaway's Palazzo Ossigeno
Iaria's Italian Restaurant
Milano Inn
The Old Spaghetti Factory

Mexican
Acapulco Joe's Mexican Foods
El Sol de Tala Mexican Restaurante
   y Cantina

Pizza
Bazbeaux Pizza
Bearno's Pizza
Eh! Formaggio

Seafood
Hot Tuna Seafood Restaurant
The Oceanaire Seafood Room

Steaks
Morton's of Chicago
Mo's A Place For Steaks
Ruth's Chris Steak House
St. Elmo Steak House
Shula's Steak House

Turkish
The Bosphorus

The Alpha List: Location, Hours, Price

Average entrée prices: $ = $10 *or less.* $$ = $10-$20. $$$ = $20 *or more.*

Acapulco Joe's Mexican Foods, 365 N. Illinois St., 637-5160. **M-20.** Long-time local establishment popular with lunchtime crowd. Open all day. $.

Aesop's Tables, 600 Massachusetts Av., 631-0055, **M-6.** Lunch and dinner Mon-Sat. Closed Sun. $$.

Agio, 635 Massachusetts Av., 488-0359, **M-6.** Dinner daily, brunch Sun. $$$.

Amici's Downtown Italian Restaurant, 601 E. New York St., 634-0440, **M-10.** Dinner Tues-Sun. $$.

Bazbeaux Pizza, 334 Massachusetts Av., 636-7662, **M-12.** Lunch and dinner daily. $.

Bertolini's Authentic Trattoria, SE cnr Maryland & Illinois Sts. (Circle Centre), 638-1800, **M-25.** Lunch and dinner daily. $$.

Bistro Tchopstix, 251 N. Illinois St., 636-9000, **M-20.** Lunch and dinner Mon-Fri, dinner only Sat. Closed Sun. $$.

The Bosphorus, 935 S. East St., 974-1770, **M-30.** Lunch and dinner Tues-Sun. $$.

Bourbon Street Distillery, 361 Indiana Av., 636-3316, **M-18.** Lunch and dinner daily. $.

Buca di Beppo, 35 N. Illinois St., 632-2822, **M-20.** Lunch and dinner daily. $$.

Chammps Americana, SE cnr Maryland & Illinois Sts. (Circle Centre), 951-0033, **M-25.** Lunch and dinner daily. $$.

Circle City Bar & Grille, 350 W. Maryland St. (in the Marriott Downtown Hotel), 405-6100, **M-22.** Breakfast, lunch, and dinner Mon-Fri. Breakfast/brunch only Sat-Sun. $$.

City Café, 443 N. Pennsylvania St., 833-2233, **M-8**. The ringer on this list—no dinner service. Breakfast Mon-Sat, lunch Mon-Fri. $.

The Claddagh Irish Pub, 234 S. Meridian St., 822-6274, **M-25**. Lunch and dinner daily. $$.

Dunaway's Palazzo Ossigeno, 351 S. East St., 638-7663, **M-23**. Lunch and dinner Mon-Fri. Dinner only Sat-Sun. $$$.

The Eagle's Nest Restaurant, 1 S. Capitol Av. (atop Hyatt Regency Hotel), 231-7566, **M-26**. Dinner daily. Reservations. $$$.

Eh! Formaggio, 30 E. Georgia St., 822-4339, M-25. Lunch and dinner Mon-Sat, closed Sun. $.

El Sol de Tala Mexican Restaurante y Cantina, Union Station, 636-8252, **M-25**. Lunch and dinner daily. $.

The Elbow Room Pub & Deli, 605 N. Pennsylvania St., 635-3354, **M-8**. Lunch and dinner daily. $.

Elements, 415 N. Alabama St., 634-8888, **M-7**. Lunch Mon-Fri, dinner Tues-Sat. Reservations. $$.

Greek Islands Restaurant, 906 S. Meridian St., 636-0700, **M-32**. Lunch Mon-Fri, dinner Mon-Sat. $.

Hard Rock Café, 49 S. Meridian St., 636-2550, **M-25**. Lunch and dinner daily. $.

Hard Times Café, 121 W. Maryland St., 916-8800, **M-26**. Lunch and dinner daily. $.

Hot Tuna Seafood Restaurant, 40 W. Jackson Pl. (in Omni Severin Hotel), 687-5190, **M-25**. Breakfast, lunch, and dinner daily. $$.

Iaria's Italian Restaurant, 317 S. College Av., 638-7706, **M-23**. Lunch Tues-Fri, dinner Tues-Sat. $$.

India Garden Restaurant, 143 N. Illinois St., 634-6060, **M-20**. Lunch and dinner, Mon-Sat. $.

Malibu on Maryland, 14 W. Maryland St., 635-4334, **M-25.** Lunch Mon-Fri, dinner daily. $$$.

Mikado Japanese Restaurant & Sushi Bar, 148 S. Illinois St., 972-4180, **M-26.** Lunch and dinner Mon-Sat. Dinner only Sun. $$$.

Milano Inn, 231 S. College Av., 264-3585, **M-23.** Lunch and dinner Mon-Sat. Dinner only Sun. $$.

Mo's A Place For Steaks. 47 S. Pennsylvania St. (corner of Maryland), 624-0720, **M-24.** Dinner Mon-Sat. Reservations. Valet parking. $$$.

Morton's of Chicago—The Steak House. 41 E. Washington St. (corner of Pennsylvania), 229-4700, **M-25.** Dinner daily. Reservations. Valet parking. $$$.

Nordstrom Grill, 130 S. Meridian St., 636-2121, **M-25.** Lunch and dinner Mon-Sat (until 7 p.m.), Sun, 12 noon to 5:30 p.m. $

The Oceanaire Seafood Room, 30 S. Meridian St., 955-2277, **M-25.** Lunch Mon-Fri, dinner daily. Reservations. Valet parking. $$$.

Old Point Tavern, 401 Massachusetts Av., 634-8943, **M-7.** Lunch and dinner Mon-Sat, dinner only Sun. $.

The Old Spaghetti Factory, 210 S. Meridian St., 635-6325, **M-25.** Lunch and dinner daily. $.

P.F. Chang's China Bistro, SE cnr Washington & Illinois Sts. (Circle Centre), 974-5747, **M-25.** Lunch and dinner daily. $$.

Palomino Restaurant Rotisseria Bar, NE cnr Maryland & Illinois Sts., 974-0400, **M-25.** Lunch Mon-Sat, dinner daily. Reservations. $$$.

Payton's Place, 551 Indiana Av., 822-8075, **M-19.** Lunch and dinner Mon-Fri, dinner Sat. $.

Ralph's Great Divide, 743 E. New York St., 637-2192, **M-9.** Lunch and dinner Mon-Fri. $.

R *Bistro*, 888 Massachusetts Av., 423-0312, **M-1**. Lunch M-F, dinner Wed-Sat. Reservations. $$.

The Rathskeller Restaurant, 401 E. Michigan St., 636-0396, **M-7**. Lunch Mon-Fri, dinner daily. $$.

The Restaurant at the Canterbury, 123 S. Illinois St., 634-3000, **M-25**. Breakfast, lunch, and dinner daily. $$$.

Rock Bottom Restaurant & Brewery, 10 W. Washington St., 681-8180, **M-20**. Lunch and dinner daily. $.

Ruth's Chris Steak House, 45 S. Illinois St. (Circle Centre), 633-1313, **M-25**. Dinner daily. $$$.

Scholars Inn Gourmet Café & Wine Bar, 725 Massachusetts Av., 536-0707, **M-6**. Lunch and dinner Tues-Fri, dinner only Sat, brunch and dinner Sun. Closed Mon. Reservations. $$.

St. Elmo Steak House, 127 S. Illinois St. (next to Canterbury Hotel), 635-0636, **M-25**. Dinner daily. Reservations. $$$.

745 Bar & Grill, 745 Massachusetts Av., 964-0102. **M-6** $

Shula's Steak House, 50 S. Capitol Av. (in the Westin Hotel), 231-3900, **M-22**. Breakfast, lunch, and dinner daily. $$$.

Slippery Noodle Inn, 372 S. Meridian St., 631-6974, **M-25**. The celebrated oldest bar downtown. Lunch Mon-Fri, lunch and dinner Sat, dinner only Sun. Must be 21. $.

Yats, 659 Massachusetts Av., 686-6380, **M-6**. Lunch and dinner Mon-Sat. $.

The Author's Favorite Restaurant List, to Date

The author and his spouse (who is a very good cook, incidentally) like the following places because food and service are consistently good, and the price/value equation seems right.

- ◎ Amici, neighborhood Italian
- ◎ Bazbeaux, pizza like no other
- ◎ City Café, for breakfast
- ◎ Elements, for innovation and style
- ◎ Nordstrom Grill, shoppers' lunch
- ◎ The Oceanaire Seafood Room, nice catch
- ◎ Old Point Tavern, for sitting outside
- ◎ Palomino, powerful atmosphere
- ◎ R Bistro, always fresh and interesting
- ◎ Scholars Inn Gourmet Café & Wine Bar, comfort zone

What do you think? Let us know how you like these places—and nominate your favorites, too. Send us a note at lvndntn@yahoo.com.

CHAPTER 5

Cheering the Team

Everybody knows Indy as the auto racing capital of the world.

Almost everybody knows Indy as the amateur sports capital of America.

But sports fans who live downtown know the most satisfying part of all—they're just minutes away from some of the best sports viewing in the U.S., and there's something going on all year long.

This chapter shows you how to connect with the sports venues downtown and nearby, including floor plans to help you select seats. Besides arranging dates with the high-profile pro teams—the NBA Indiana Pacers and the NFL Indianapolis Colts—use this chapter to plan an outing with the Indianapolis Indians, farm team of the Milwaukee Brewers; the Indiana Fever, an Eastern Conference team of the WNBA; the Indianapolis Firebirds AFL football team; and the Indianapolis Ice hockey team. And as a bonus on the pro side, this chapter also contains the layout of the Indianapolis Motor Speedway. So, start your engines!

Collegiate and amateur sports are well represented in downtown Indy. During the next few years your choices include:

◎ The Big Ten Men's and Women's Basketball Tournaments.
◎ NCAA Division I Women's Basketball Championship—the Final Four.
◎ The U.S.A. Gymnastics National Championships.
◎ The NCAA Division I Men's Basketball Championship—the Final Four—at the RCA Dome.

Conseco Fieldhouse

125 S. Pennsylvania St., **M-24**

www.ConsecoFieldhouse.com

Indiana Pacers basketball team (NBA) 917-2727

Indiana Fever basketball team (WNBA) 917-2727

Indiana Firebirds arena football team (AFL) 472-8080

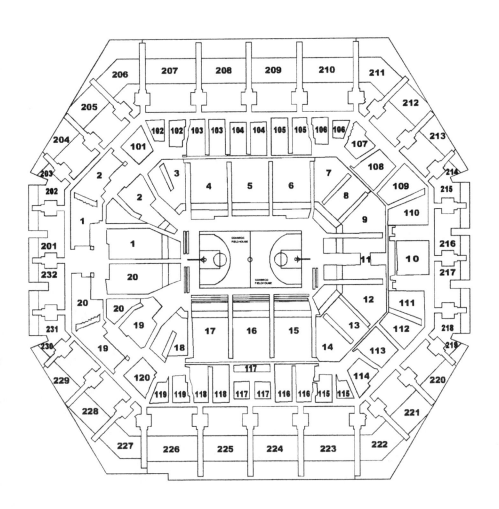

RCA Dome

100 S. Capitol Av., **M-26**

Indianapolis Colts football team (NFL), 297-7000, www.colts.com

Football Setup

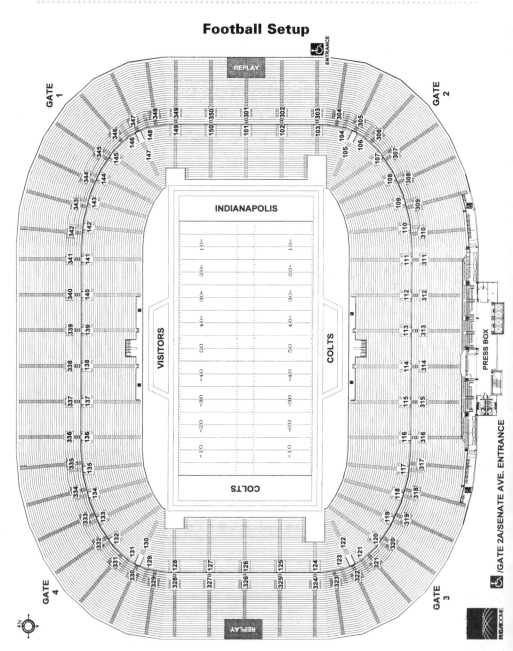

RCA Dome

Basketball Setup

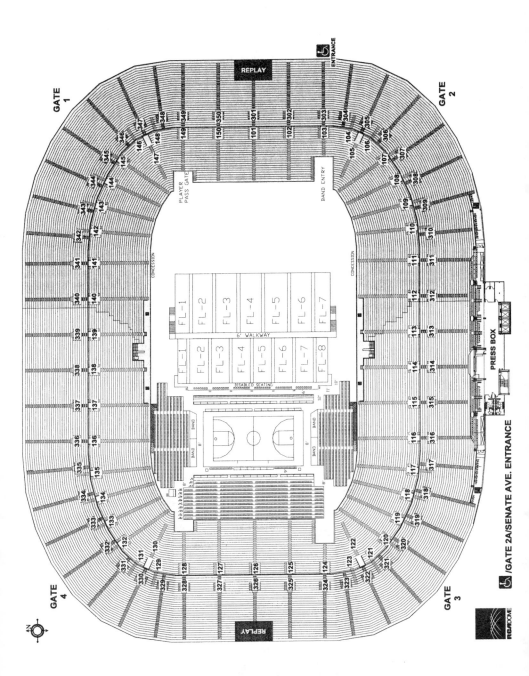

Victory Field

501 W. Maryland St., **M-27**

Indianapolis Indians baseball team, International League,

Milwaukee Brewers affiliate,

www.indyindians.com

Season and group tickets, 269-3545. Daily tickets, 239-5151.

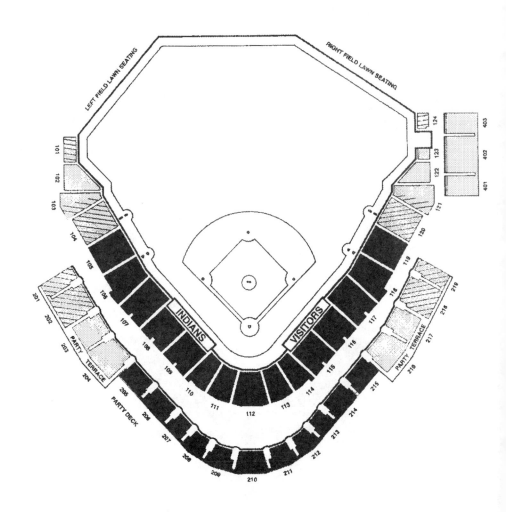

Pepsi Coliseum

1202 E. 38th St.

Indianapolis Ice hockey team, www.indianapolisice.com, 925-4423

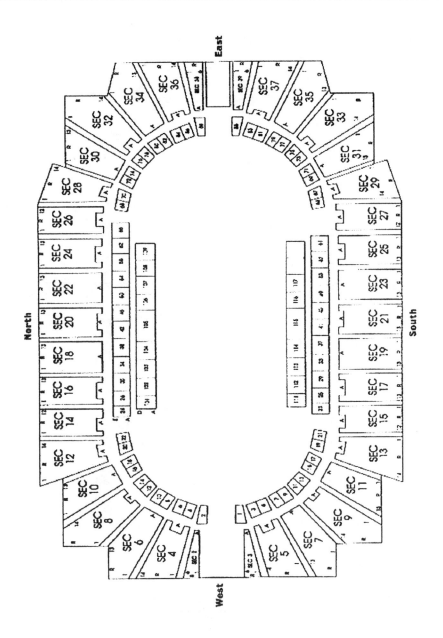

Indianapolis Motor Speedway

www.brickyard.com

4790 W. 16th St., 492-6700, www.imstix.com

Indianapolis 500, Indy Racing League, Memorial Day weekend

Brickyard 400, NASCAR

United States Grand Prix

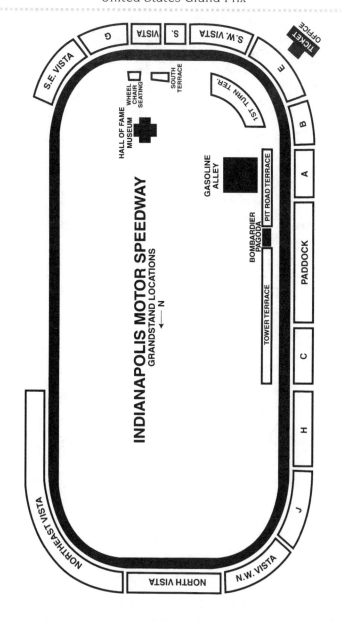

Show Time!

Downtown Indy contains four major performing halls and three smaller spaces. This chapter shows you the floor plans for all seven venues so you'll know where you're sitting when you order tickets. In alphabetical order, the places are:

- American Cabaret Theatre
- Hilbert Circle Theatre
- Indiana Repertory Theatre
- Madame Walker Theatre Center
- Murat Centre
- Phoenix Theatre
- Theatre on the Square

But you don't need reservations to script your own night of entertainment, for example, popping around two of the Cultural Districts—Massachusetts Avenue and the Wholesale District. Possible itineraries:

Mass Avenue

Shopping is the soul of entertainment, so start late afternoon at the far northeast end (**M-1**), at Teapots Flea Market. Then schmooze through the galleries on Mass Avenue. By now it's 6-6:30 p.m. Have a drink at Scholar's Inn (**M-6**), then walk next door for the first show at ComedySportz Arena. Hungry? The following block offers choices from all around the globe—Yats, Agio, Aesop's Tables. Sprint past Fire Station No. 7 and ride some riffs at the Chatterbox Jazz Club (**M-7**), sip a cappuccino at Starbuck's.

Wholesale District

Map **M-25** shows you the whole scene. Start at the Slippery Noodle Inn (South & Meridian Sts.)—or end there, it's a national landmark. Drop in at Crackers Comedy Club, check out Jillian's, Claddagh Irish Pub, Hot Tuna at the Omni Severin Hotel, or Eh! Formaggio (the most emphatic pizza joint west of New York) Close the evening in style: become a nighthawk at the Red Eye Café, use your imagination.

American Cabaret Theatre

www.americancabarettheatre.com,
401 E. Michigan St., 631-0334, **M-7**

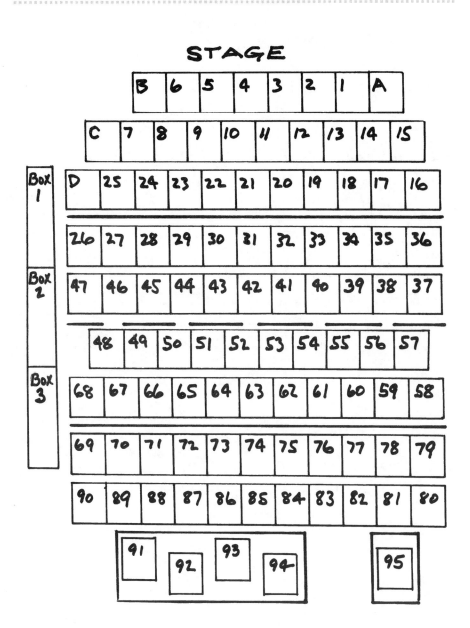

STAGE

Hilbert Circle Theatre

Indianapolis Symphony Orchestra, www.indyorch.org,
45 Monument Circle, 639-4300, **M-20**

Main Floor

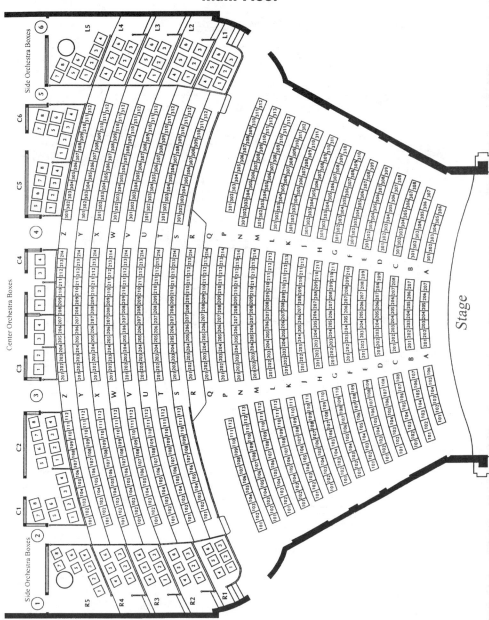

Hilbert Circle Theatre

Balcony

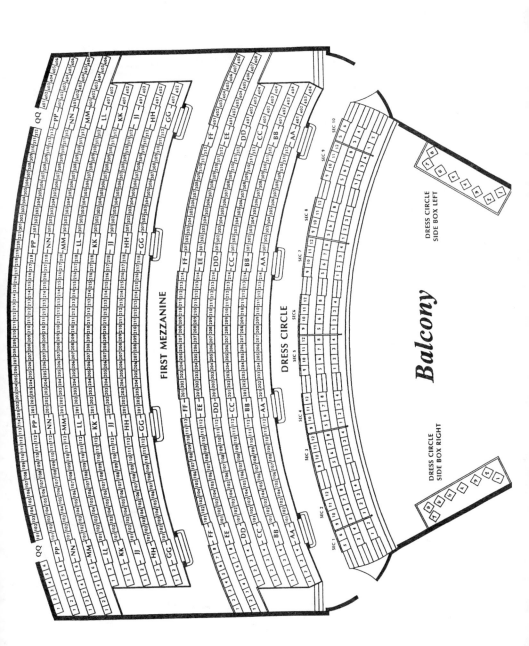

Hilbert Circle Theatre

Stage

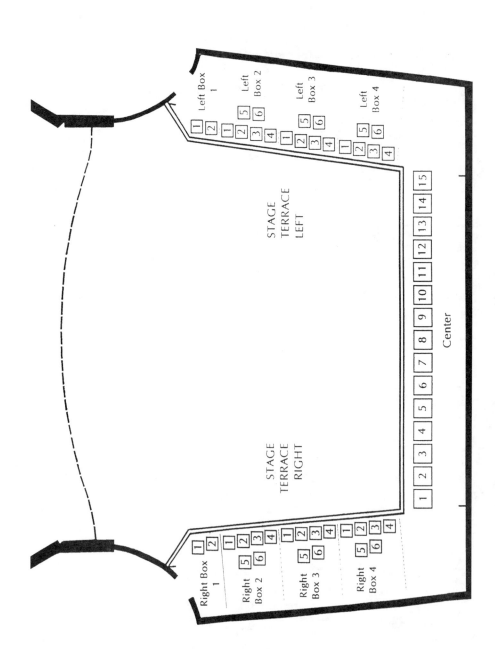

Indiana Repertory Theatre

www.indianarep.com

140 W. Washington St., 635-5252, **M-21**

Main Stage

STAGE

ODD
LEFT

EVEN
RIGHT

CENTER

MAIN FLOOR

MEZZANINE

Indiana Repertory Theatre, Upper Stage

Upper Stage

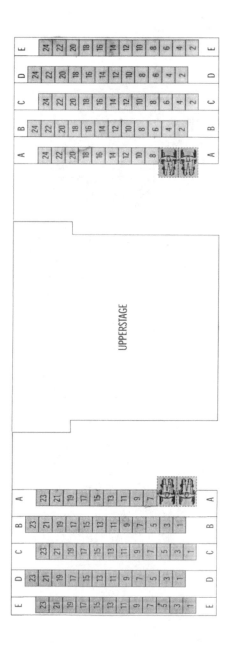

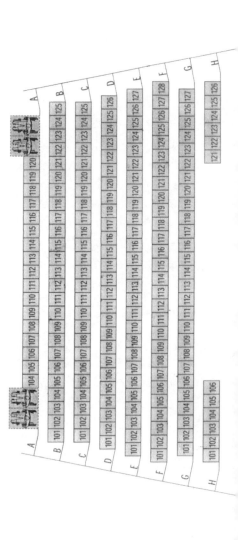

Madame Walker Theatre Center

www.walkertheatre.com,
617 Indiana Av., 236-2099, **M-19**

Main Floor

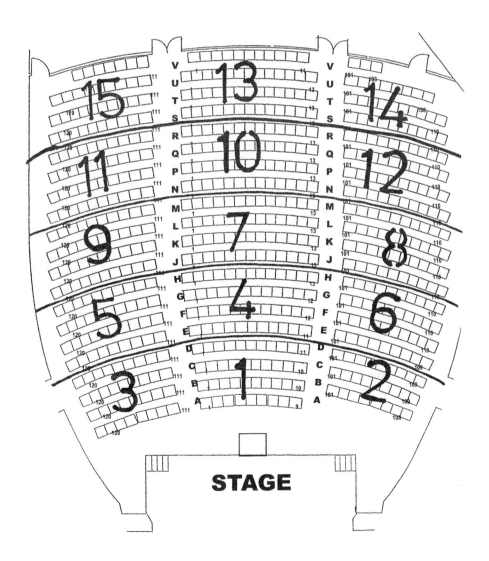

STAGE

Madame Walker Theatre Center

Balcony

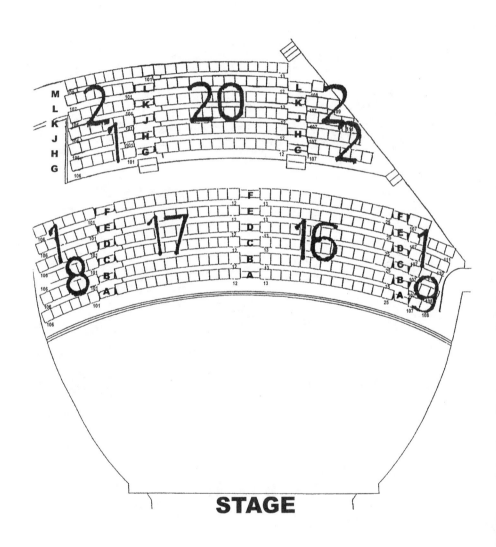

STAGE

Murat Theatre

www.murat.com,
502 N. New Jersey St., 231-0000, **M-7**
Many Broadway Shows come here—check newspapers
Ballet Internationale – Indianapolis, 637-8979

Main Floor

STAGE

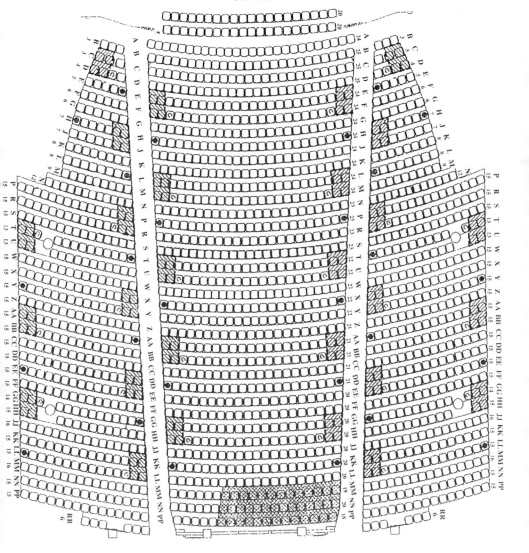

Murat Theatre

Balcony

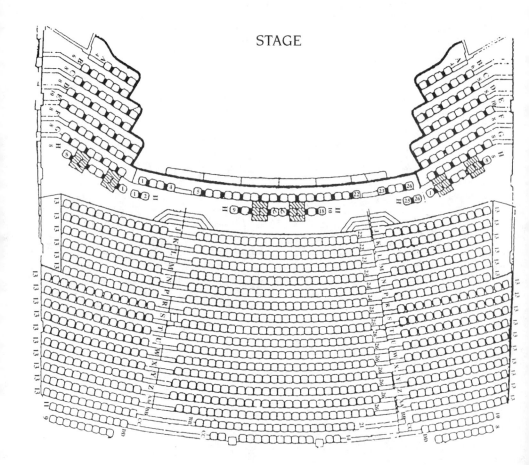

STAGE

Phoenix Theatre

www.phoenixtheatre.org,

749 N. Park Av., 635-7529, **M-6**

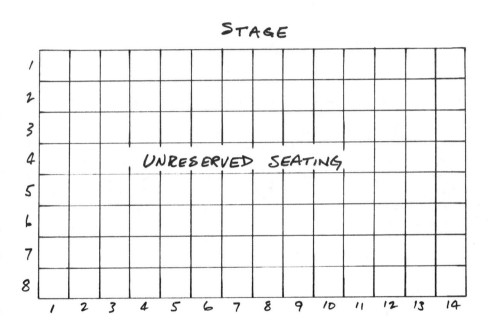

Theatre on the Square

www.tots.org

627 Massachusetts Av., 637-8085, M-6

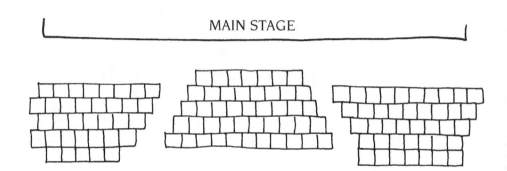

MAIN STAGE

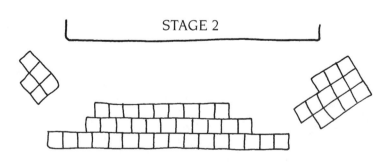

STAGE 2

CHAPTER 7

Staying Healthy, Top to Toe

One tough task when you move to a new home territory is finding a new group of specialists to take care of your aching body, or to simply offer periodic reassurance that you're doing OK inside your skin. Good news: Living in downtown Indy, you are within walking distance, or a very short drive, of doctors, dentists, psychologists, psychiatrists, podiatrists, and virtually every other physical-mental specialty. You have no excuse for not receiving very good care, should the need arise.

Many health-care providers have offices downtown—in the shadow of Monument Circle, so to speak (see the list later in this chapter). Many more have offices at the IUPUI campus (**M-28**), home of IU Medical School, second largest in the country. It may not have occurred to you to seek ordinary, check-up style health care in a hospital setting, but you can do exactly that in various departments of Indiana University Hospital (550 University Blvd., 916-3525), Wishard Memorial Hospital (1001 W. 10th St., 639-6671), Riley Hospital for Children (702 Barnhill Dr., 274-4862); or, less than a mile north of downtown, at Methodist Hospital (1701 Senate Blvd., 916-3525).

This collection of nationally-respected health-care providers is a key factor in Indy's ranking as one of the best U.S. cities overall for quality of life. In the Millennium Edition of *Places Rated Almanac*, published in 2000, Indianapolis ranks 23rd nationally, keeping company with places like New Orleans, ranked 21, and Orlando, 22. (Come to think of it, Indy does have touches of Mardi Gras and Disney.)

If you're finicky about choosing a new internist, OB/GYN, or other specialist and wish to reveal yourself only to a recognized expert, the biennial "Top Doctors" survey conducted by *Indianapolis Monthly* may give you some leads. Back issues of the magazine are available at the Interim Central Library, 202 N. Alabama St., 269-1700. Some of the docs on the magazine's list have offices downtown and many have affiliations with the downtown hospitals.

Assembling Your New Team of Health-Care Providers

The following pages contain lists of health care providers, beginning with dentists in practice downtown. Note in the dentists list that your choices even include a dental school—the Indiana University School of Dentistry, on the IUPUI campus. The bold **M** numbers indicate the map page for location.

Downtown Dentists

Bierman, Gregory, DDS, 201 N. Illinois St., Suite 1770, 237-2225, **M-20**

Brite Smile Center, 49 W. Maryland St, 964-0423, **M-25**

Crow, Lora L., DDS, 201 N. Illinois St., Suite 1770, 237-2225, **M-20**

Downtown Dental Group, PC, 201 N. Illinois St., Suite 1770, 237-2225, **M-20**

Draheim, Susan E., DDS, 29 E. McCarty St., Bldg. B, 684-1997, **M-32**

Erickson, Jon, DDS, 201 N. Illinois St., Suite 1770, 237-2225, **M-20**

Erotas, Edward, DDS, 1 American Square (AUL Bldg.), 955-3988, **M-21**

Hovey, Cynthia, DDS, 303 N. Alabama St., 637-4636, **M-11**

Indiana University School of Dentistry, 1121 W. Michigan St. General Information, 274-7957; Adult Patients-Student Clinics, 274-7433; Child Patients-Student Clinics, 274-8111; Dental Faculty Private Practice Patients, 274-5628, **M-28**

Kilgore, David J., DDS, 320 N. Meridian St., 632-6258, **M-20**

Marshall, William K., DDS, 10 W. Market St., 639-3523, **M-20**

Midwest Periodontal & Oral Reconstruction, 502 Indiana Av., 269-0402, **M-19**

Mills, Ryan, DDS, 201 N. Illinois St., Suite 1770, 237-2225, **M-20**

Phillips, Timothy B., DDS, Bank One Building, 111 Monument Circle, 632-1488, **M-20**

Sabir-Holloway, Jeannette, 502 Indiana Av., 269-0402, **M-19**

Sherer, Richard E., DDS, 151 N. Delaware St., 634-8440, **M-12**

Taube, Jane E., DDS, 320 N. Meridian St., 632-6258, **M-20**

Taube, Jennifer A., DDS, 320 N. Meridian St., 632-6201, **M-20**

Taylor, Todd, DDS, 201 N. Illinois St., Suite 1770, 237-2225, **M-20**

Downtown Physicians & Surgeons

Some of the physicians and surgeons included in the following lists have their offices about a mile north of downtown Indy, in the cluster of medical facilities between 16th and 20th streets and Capitol Avenue and Senate Boulevard. From downtown, Senate Avenue and Illinois Street lead directly to the area.

Allergy & Immunology

Allergy & Asthma Care of Indiana, 1815 N. Capitol Av., 925-3533

Baker, William, MD, 550 N. University Blvd., 274-8660, **M-28**

Houser, D. Duane, MD, 550 N. University Blvd, 274-8660, **M-28**

Indiana University Asthma & Allergy Center, 550 N. University Blvd., 274-8660, **M-28**

Jansen, Noel L., MD, 1815 N. Capitol Av., 925-3533

Kelkar, Pramod S., MD, 1815 N. Capitol Av., 925-3533

Cardiology

Batties, Paul Terry, MD, 1633 N. Capitol Av., 924-1001

Care Group at Methodist Hospital, 1801 N. Senate Blvd., 924-5444

IU Cardiac Rehabilitation, 250 University Blvd., 274-4482, **M-28**

Krannert Institute of Cardiology, 1801 N. Senate Blvd, 962-0500

Dermatology

Dermatology, Inc., 1801 Senate Blvd., Suite 745, 926-3739

Indiana University Dermatology, 550 N. University Blvd., 274-7744, **M-28**

Endocrinology

Indiana University Endocrinology, 550 N. University Blvd., 274-8660, **M-28**

Osteoporosis Care Center, 550 N. University Blvd., 274-8660, **M-28**

Family Practice

Indiana University-Methodist Family Practice Center, 1520 N. Senate Av., 962-8893

Lockerbie Family Practice, 303 N. Alabama St. (Lockerbie Marketplace), 916-9946, **M-11**

Massachusetts Avenue Medical Group, 342 Massachusetts Av., 638-1851, **M-12**

Gastroenterology

Blitz, Gregory P., MD, 1801 N. Senate Blvd., 962-6300

Brown, David N., MD, 1801 N. Senate Blvd., 962-6300

Gordon, O.T., MD, 1801 N. Senate Blvd., 962-6300

Indiana University Gastroenterology/Hepatology Group, 550 N. University Blvd., 274-8660, **M-28**

Jain, Ajay, MD, 1801 N. Senate Blvd., 962-6300

Meisenheimer, Martin P., MD, 1801 N. Senate Blvd., 962-6300

Meridian Endoscopy Center, 1801 N. Senate Blvd., 962-5660

Meridian Medical Group, PC, 1801 N. Senate Blvd., 962-6300

Odelowo, Olajide, MD, 1801 N. Senate Blvd., 962-6300

Thomas, David B., MD, 1801 N. Senate Blvd., 962-6300

Whitmore, Robert T., MD, 1801 N. Senate Blvd., 962-6300

General Surgery

Tower Surgical, Inc., 1801 N. Senate Blvd., Suite 635, 923-7211

Geriatrics

Center for Geriatric Medicine, 1633 N. Capitol Av., 962-2929

IU Center for Senior Health, 1001 W. 10th St., 630-8000, **M-28**

Gynecology

Benson, J. Thomas, MD, 1633 N. Capitol Av., 962-6600

Hale, Douglas S., MD, 1633 N. Capitol Av., 962-6600

Meridian Gynecological Center, 324 E. New York St., 831-9469, **M-11**

Mutone, Martina F., 1633 N. Capitol Av., 962-6600

Saini, Jyot, MD, 550 N. University Blvd., 274-8231, **M-28**

Schoon, Paul G., MD, 550 N. University Blvd., 274-8231, **M-28**

Soper, Mary E., MD, 1801 N. Senate Blvd., 963-0383

Urogynecology Associates, 1633 N. Capitol Av., 962-6600

Valaitis, Sandra, MD, 550 N. University Blvd., 274-8231, **M-28**

Hand Surgery

Cohen, Adam C., MD, 1001 W. 10th St., 630-7429, **M-28**

Qazi, Haroon M., MD, 1935 N. Capitol Av., 923-4822

Hematology

Hematology-Oncology, 1633 N. Capitol Av., Suite 300, 927-0825

Methodist Cancer Center, 1701 N. Senate Blvd., 962-8288

Infectious Disease

Indiana University Infectious Diseases Group, 550 N. University Blvd., 274-8660, **M-28**

Israel, Karen, MD, 1633 N. Capitol Av., 962-2424

Internal Medicine

IU Medical Group – Primary Care, 550 N. University Blvd., 692-2300, **M-28**

Indiana University Internists, 550 N. University Blvd., 274-8660, **M-28**

Johnson, Michael T., MD, 550 N. University Blvd., 274-8660, **M-28**

Pettigrew, Timothy J., 550 N. University Blvd., 274-8660, **M-28**

Nephrology

Indiana University Nephrologists, 950 W. Walnut St., 274-8660, **M-28**

Nephrology and Internal Medicine, Inc., 1801 N. Senate Blvd., Suite 355, 924-8425

Neurological Surgery

Indianapolis Neurosurgical Group, Inc., 1801 Senate Av., 396-1300

Indiana University Neurology (adult and child), 545 Barnhill Dr., 274-2372, **M-28**

University Neurosurgical Associates, Inc. Adult Services: 545 Barnhill Dr., 274-8422, **M-28;** Pediatric Services, Riley Hospital, Room 1730, 274-8852, **M-28**

Neurology

Hoosier Neurology, PC, 1801 N. Senate Blvd., Suite 510, 962-5828

Obstetrics & Gynecology

Coleman Center for Women, 550 N. University Blvd., 274-8231, **M-28**

Fox, David, MD, 1633 N. Capitol Av., 962-0667

Fehd, Karla, MD, 1801 N. Senate Blvd., 890-5596

Indiana University Obstetrics & Gynecology, 550 N. University Blvd., 274-8231, **M-28**

Methodist Hospital Labor & Delivery, 1701 N. Senate Blvd., 962-343

Soper, Mary E., MD, 1801 N. Senate Blvd., 963-0383

University Obstetricians-Gynecologists, Inc., 550 N. University Blvd., 274-8231, **M-28**

Weber, Brad, MD, 1604 N. Capitol Av., 216-2400

Occupational Medicine

Indiana University Corporate Health & Wellness Services, 250 University Blvd., 274-8580, **M-28**

Oncology

Hematology-Oncology, 1633 N. Capitol Av., Suite 300, 927-0825

Indiana University Hematology/Oncology, 535 Barnhill Dr., 274-0920, **M-28**

IU Cancer Center, 535 Barnhill Dr., 278-4822, **M-28**

Methodist Radiation Oncology Center, 1701 N. Senate Blvd., 962-3172

Methodist Cancer Center, 1701 N. Senate Blvd., 962-8288

Ophthalmology

Abrams, John H., MD, 1801 N. Senate Blvd., 926-6699

Eye Specialists of Indiana, 1901 N. Meridian St., 925-2200

Indiana University Ophthalmology, IU Hospital & Outpatient Center, 3rd Floor,
550 N. University Blvd., 274-4416, **M-28**

Lloyd, Betty-Jo Rawles, MD, 1801 N. Senate Blvd., 926-6699

Midwest Eye Institute, 702 Barnhill Dr., 274-8103, **M-28**

Walton, Paul L., MD, 1901 N. Meridian St., 925-2200

Orthopedic Surgery

Baele, Joseph R., MD, 1801 N. Senate Blvd., 917-4365

Brokaw, David S., MD, 1801 N. Senate Blvd., 917-4396

Carlson, Dwayne A., MD, 1801 N. Senate Blvd., 917-4392

Coscia, Michael F., MD, 1801 N. Senate Blvd., 917-4390

Dietz, John W. Jr., MD, 1801 N. Senate Blvd., 802-2000

Fisher, David A., MD, 1801 N. Senate Blvd., 917-4365

Huler, Robert J., MD, 1801 N. Senate Blvd., 917-4394

IU Orthopedics & Sports Medicine: Adult Appointments, University Hospital,
550 N. University Blvd., Room 1250, 278-4501, **M-28**;
Pediatric Appointments, Riley Hospital, 702 Barnhill Dr., Room 1300,
274-4315, **M-28**

Jelen, Bradley O., DO, 1801 N. Senate Blvd., 917-4394

Kaehr, David S., MD, 1801 N. Senate Blvd., 917-4396

Maar, Dean C., MD, 1801 N. Senate Blvd., 917-4390

Methodist Sports Medicine Center, 1815 N. Capitol Av., 924-8600

OrthoIndy, 1801 N. Senate Blvd., 923-5352

Scheid, D. Kevin, MD, 1801 N. Senate Blvd., 917-4390

Schwartz, David G., MD, 1801 N. Senate Blvd., 917-4392

Trammell, Terry R., MD, 1801 N. Senate Blvd., 917-4365

Vicar, Andrew J., MD, 1801 N. Senate Blvd., 917-4394

Weber, Timothy G., MD, 1801 N. Senate Blvd., 917-4392

Otology & Neurotology

IU Otolaryngology, 702 Barnhill Dr., 274-3556, **M-28**

Otorhinolaryngology (Ear, Nose & Throat)
    Head & Neck Center at Methodist Hospital, 1633 N. Capitol Av., 962-0333
    Head & Neck Surgery Associates, PC, 1633 N. Capitol Av., Suite 300, 926-1056
    University Otolaryngology Associates, Inc., 702 Barnhill Dr., 274-3556, **M-28**

Pediatric
    Corbitt, Toya, MD, 1815 N. Capitol Av., 925-7795
    Methodist Children's Pavilion, 1701 N. Senate Blvd., 962-2000
    Riley Hospital for Children, 702 Barnhill Dr., 274-5000, **M-28**
    Yancy, Eric A., MD, 1815 N. Capitol Av., 925-7795

Pediatric Allergies
    Kelkar, Pramod S., MD, 1815 N. Capitol Av., 925-3533

Pediatric Surgery
    IU Orthopedics and Sports Medicine, 702 Barnhill Dr., Room 1300, 274-4365,
        M-28
    Riley Pediatric Urology, 702 Barnhill Dr., 274-8896, **M-28**

Plastic, Reconstructive & Cosmetic Surgery
    Cohen, Adam C., MD, 1001 W. 10th St., 630-7429, **M-28**
    Coleman, John J. III, MD, 545 Barnhill Dr., 274-8106, **M-28**
    Eppley, Barry L., MD, 702 Barnhill Dr., 274-8106, **M-28**
    Havlik, Robert J., MD, 702 Barnhill Dr., 274-2430, **M-28**
    Plastic Surgery Center of Indiana, PC, 1935 N. Capitol Av., 923-4822
    Sadove, A. Michael, MD, 702 Barnhill Dr., 274-3778, **M-28**

Psychiatry
    IU Medical Group Adult Psychiatry Services, 278-4344
    Davis Clinic, PC, 1431 N. Delaware St., 635-0335

Pulmonary Diseases
    IU Cardiac & Pulmonary Rehabilitation, 250 University Blvd., 274-4482, M-28
    IU Pulmonary, Allergy, Critical Care & Occupational Medicine, 550 N. University
        Blvd., 274-8660, **M-28**

Radiology
   Indiana University Radiology Associates, 550 N. University Blvd., 274-2881, **M-28**

Reproductive Endocrinology
   University Obstetricians-Gynecologists, Inc., 550 N. University Blvd., 274-4875,
      M-28

Rheumatology
   Arthritis Care Center, 1801 N. Senate Blvd., 962-3500
   IU Rheumatology Group, 550 N. University Blvd., 274-8660, **M-28**

Sleep Disorders
   IU Sleep Disorder Center, 550 N. University Blvd., 274-8660, **M-28**

Sports Medicine
   Methodist Sports Medicine Center, 1815 N. Capitol Av., 924-8600

Thoracic Surgery
   Cardiothoracic Surgeons, Inc., 545 Barnhill Dr., 274-7150, **M-28**
   Corvasc, Methodist Professional Center, 1801 N. Senate Blvd., Suite 755,
      923-1787
   Kesler, Kenneth M., MD, 545 Barnhill Dr., 274-2394, **M-28**
   Mahomed, Yousuf, MD, 1801 N. Senate Blvd., 962-0250
   Meldrum, Daniel R., MD, 1801 N. Senate Blvd., 962-0250
   Methodist Heart Station, 1701 N. Senate Blvd., 962-8447

Urology
   Institute for Kidney Stone Disease, 1801 N. Senate Blvd., 927-8663
   Methodist Urology, LLC, 1801 N. Senate Blvd., 962-3700
   University Urologists, PC, Inc., 535 Barnhill Dr., 274-7451, **M-28**

Vascular Surgery
   University Vascular, 1801 N. Senate Blvd., 962-0281

Staying in Shape Downtown

And now for a sweeping generalization that's completely unsupported by scientific evidence: Downtowners are in better shape than suburbanites.

The basis of that bold assertion is nothing more substantial than observing the downtown scene for a couple of years and attending numerous gatherings of downtown residents. You don't see as many full-figured folks. My neighbors in the condo certainly are a slim, young crowd.

Just a guess, but the reason that downtowners of all ages appear in better shape could be that exercise is a part of everyday downtown life, whether you are into exercise or not. Consider the simple matter of walking rather than driving. Walking is an option downtown because of sidewalks—on both sides of most streets. Walking isn't an option in many suburbs because of distance, of course, but also for lack of sidewalks. On the other hand, driving downtown can be a hassle if you can't find a quick-cheap place to park. When you live downtown, it may be faster and easier to walk than to drive.

Stair-climbing is another built-in feature of downtown life. Apartment and condo residents have lots of stairs in their everyday routine. Anyone lurking around Monument Circle, the War Memorial, or the Federal Courthouse must be sorely tempted to climb the stairs, just for the fun of it.

Running? Yes, running may also be more common downtown than in the suburbs, even if you're not a runner. People run downtown when they're caught in a downpour while walking.

The point is that living downtown can get you into better physical shape even if shaping up is not on your agenda. But if staying in shape *is* on your agenda and you enjoy keeping fit, you are doubly rewarded downtown by (1) the exercise that simply comes with the territory and (2) all sorts of opportunities for the exercise you really enjoy. This chapter shows you how to indulge your sensible passions.

Walking/Running/Biking/Swimming/Tennis

Canal Walk

Canal Walk (see maps **M-15, M-19, M-22, M-27**) is a very popular promenade for downtown residents, office workers, and visitors. From the headwaters at 11th Street to the confluence with the White River, the canal length is 1.47 miles. You can also pedal-boat the canal and ride a family-size bike on the walk (see Directory).

Monon Trail

Known formally as the Monon Rail-Trail of Indy Parks Greenways, this splendid hiking-biking path begins on the north side of 10th Street in the middle of the I-65/I-70 loop at the northeast corner of downtown (see map **M-1**). That may sound like a very busy place, traffic-wise, but getting there is easy via sidewalks and underpasses. The Monon presently stretches about 15 miles north into Hamilton County. Of course, you can turn around and backtrack at any point. But there's an interesting alternative for returning downtown at about the six-mile point where the Monon meets the Central Canal Towpath, a route paralleling the White River southwesterly to the White River Trail, returning you to White River State Park (**M-27**). This loop measures about 16 miles.

Running the Mini-Marathon

Indianapolis Life 500 Festival Mini-Marathon
2960 N. Meridian St.
Indianapolis, IN 46208
317-614-6464
raceinfo@500festival.com

The nation's largest half-marathon (13.1 miles) was sold out at 30,000 participants in 2004. So was the shorter 5K event. If you're interested in running next year, better register today! Runners line up on Washington Street downtown and finish at Military Park (**M-27**). For Mini runners, the scenic highlight of this early-May event is looping the track at the Indianapolis Motor Speedway a few weeks before race cars do the same in the Indy 500.

Sure, the Mini is a once-a-year deal. But many runners make it a 12-month program, focusing their training on the May event. Some even perfect their running style at the National Institute for Fitness and Sport (see later in this chapter).

Swimming

Indiana University Natatorium
901 W. New York St. **(M-27)**
274-3518
www.iunat.iupui.edu

Arguably the best public swimming facility in any downtown U.S. setting, the IU Natatorium has hosted several Olympic Trials in the 50-meter competition pool. More important, the doors open every day for ordinary mortals to get in their laps and perhaps tack on some weight work, aerobics classes, or walking/running at the adjacent outdoor track.

Facilities & hours. 50-meter competition pool, 18-foot diving well, 50-meter instructional pool, two exercise rooms, quarter-mile track across the street at the IU Track & Soccer Stadium. Parking in an adjoining garage ($10 a month).

Open swimming Monday through Thursday, 5:30 a.m. to 8 p.m.; Friday, 5:30 a.m. to 7 p.m.; Sunday, 1 p.m. to 5 p.m. Weight room open same hours as open swimming plus Saturday from 9 a.m. to noon.

Lap swimming is at your own pace. No age restrictions for lap swimming but participants must be able to swim in deep water and share lanes if necessary. On Sunday afternoons, the Natatorium instructional pool is open for family swim—the water is heated to 86 degrees.

Cost. You can try out the pool and weight room one time for $6. Longer term memberships are a better deal. For the pool, a 15-visit pass costs $55; 40-visit pass, $135. Towels are 50¢.

"You can vary your fitness program and get an all-round workout by taking advantage of the pools, weight rooms, and aerobic classes at the IU Natatorium and running/walking at the IU Michael A. Carroll Track & Soccer Stadium," the IU website says. The cost of the combo deal: one month, $42; six months, $225; one year, $400. IUPUI faculty, staff, and students; state employees; and persons 60 years old and older are eligible for a 10% discount.

Tennis

Indianapolis Tennis Center
150 University Blvd. **(M-27)**
278-2100
www.sportcomplex.iupui.edu

Indianapolis Tennis Center is the only downtown tennis facility. It's open to both members and nonmembers.

Facilities & hours. 14 outdoor hard courts, 6 indoor courts, 4 Har-Tru Clay courts, private/group lessons and clinics, pro shop, men's and women's locker rooms, racquet stringing, parking. Open 6:30 a.m. to 10 p.m. Monday through Friday, 7 a.m. to 9 p.m Saturday, 8 a.m. to 9 p.m. Sunday. Group lessons are scheduled at various hours for various ages and abilities ranging from Pee Wee Tennis (age 3 to 6) to Elite II high school boys preparing for spring and summer tournaments. Contact the center for current offerings.

Cost. Annual family membership, $350; married couple, $275; individual 19 years and older, $175; juniors 18 and under, $100; seniors 60 and older, $125. Indoor court fees for members range from $12 an hour for walk-ons to $24 an hour peak times; outdoor courts for members range from $4 to $14 an hour. Nonmember hourly rates range from $18 walk-on to $34 peak times. Contact the center for current rates.

Working Out

National Institute for Fitness and Sport
250 University Blvd. **(M-27)**
274-3432
www.nifs.org

Don't let that stuffy name put you off. The National Institute for Fitness and Sport—NIFS—is a handsome, upbeat, well-equipped place where you can sweat at your own rate or tap into a wide range of expert coaching and counsel.

Facilities & hours. Members have the use of a 200-meter indoor running/walking track; an NBA size basketball court; more than 100 pieces of cardio equipment; more than 40 group fitness classes; extensive weight training equipment; individual exercise consultations with certified professional staff. Equipment checkout includes basketballs, volleyballs, security locker keys, heart rate monitors, golf clubs and balls, ping pong paddles and balls. Locker rooms include sauna, steam room, and whirlpool; and towels are provided. Hours: Monday through Thursday, 5:30 a.m. to 10 p.m.; Friday, 5:30 a.m. to 9 p.m. Saturday and Sunday, 7 a.m. to 6 p.m.

Cost. NIFS charges an initiation fee plus a monthly fee. For the full picture, take a look at the NIFS website. But for example, in 2004 the individual initiation fee was $195 and the monthly fee $51.50 under an automated payment plan. The corporate rate was initiation of $150 and monthly fee of $42.50. Reduced rates also are available for students, persons 60 and older and their spouses, and youths age 11 to 15. There is no minimum membership period, and the one-time initiation fee covers all periods of active membership. You can try NIFS for a day for $12 or a week for $30.

YMCA at the Athenaeum
401 E. Michigan St. **(M-7)**
685-9705
www.indymca.org

The downtown Y is one of six YMCA branches in the Indianapolis area, and membership in one includes access to any of the others.

Facilities & hours. Basketball for adults, teens, and youths; cardio equipment including treadmills, stair climbers, stationary bikes, and Concept II rowers; Olympic free weights; Cybex resistance equipment; non-water aerobic classes; lockers, showers, and towels (50¢ a day). The Atheneum Y also offers a wide range of Wellness Classes Monday through Saturday from early morning to evening. Hours at the Atheneum Y: Monday through Thursday, 6 a.m. to 10 p.m.; Friday, 6 a.m. to 9 p.m.; Saturday, 8 a.m. to 5 p.m.; Sunday, 12 noon to 5 p.m.

Cost. No initiation fee but a 6-month membership is the minimum term, with monthly payment by automatic bank draft or payment in full in advance. Monthly fees in 2004 were: two-adult household, $64; single adult household, $52; adult, $44; youth, $26; senior, $40; senior two-adult household, $50; senior single adult household, $540. Call for current rates.

■ ■ ■ ■ ■ ■ ■ ■ ■ ■ ■ ■ ■ ■ ■ ■ ■

For people who like the thought of exercise more than exercise itself

If you prefer to exercise your mind rather than your body, you can do so every weekday 8 a.m. to 5 p.m. at the National Art Museum of Sport at University Place, 850 W. Michigan Av., 274-3627, **M-28**. The museum houses what's believed to be the nation's largest collection of art depicting sport. Artists represented include Winslow Homer, George Bellows, LeRoy Neiman, and Ogden Pleissner. Admission is free.

Summer Sport Camps for Kids

IUPUI *Sport Complex*
901 W. New York St. **(M-27)**
278-1778
www.sportcomplex.iupui.edu

Two principal kinds of summer camps are offered at the Sport Complex just west of downtown:

Summer Day Camp is a sport-oriented, full-day camp for kids age 5 to 12. The focus is on introducing children to various sports and developing basic skills in a noncompetitive atmosphere. Sessions begin the first full week of June and run through the end of July. The daily program begins at 8:30 a.m. and ends at 4 p.m. Early drop-off and late pick-up can be arranged. The weekly fee in 2004 was $156.

Sport-specific camps are offered for boys and girls age 6 through 18. Most are week-long sessions, half day and full day. The sports are soccer, tennis, lacrosse, track & field, swimming, synchronized swimming, and diving. Prices vary. Contact the IUPUI Sport Complex for details.

Bike Rental

The Bike Shop
922 Massachusetts Av. **(M-1)**
687-8768

New in the spring of 2004, The Bike Shop is located in the garage area of Teapots 'n Treasures, a little flea market also new in '04. Ben Rossiter, a certified bike mechanic, presides over the bike rental-repair-sales business. Rentals begin at $10 an hour. Visitors can arrange for bike delivery to downtown hotels. But if you're interested in a long ride on a nice day, picking up your rental bike at the shop makes good sense because you're only a couple of minutes from the southern terminus of the Monon Rail-Trail (see map **M-1**), the 15-mile paved path running north to 146th Street, Carmel. Check these hours of business: Monday and Tuesday, noon to 6 p.m.; Thursday and Friday, 10 a.m. to 6 p.m.; Saturday, 10 a.m. to 5 p.m. and 8 p.m. to 11 p.m. The Bike Shop is closed on Sunday and Wednesday.

And Even More Choices

Curves
135 N. Pennsylvania St., Suite 110 **(M-12)**
685-8206
www.curvesinternational.com

Curves, the women's club, offers "30-minute fitness, common sense weight loss, and all of the support you need to achieve your goals."

Indiana/World Skating Academy
201 S. Capitol Av. **(M-26)**
237-5555
www.iwsa.org

The academy has both NHL and Olympic size rinks. Public skating, skate rental, and group rates available. Call for schedule.

Indianapolis Athletic Club
350 N. Meridian St. **(M-20)**
634-4331
www.iacindy.com

The clubhouse contains a 5-lane, 25-yard swimming pool; fitness center, basketball court, racquetball and squash courts. Parking garage.

Indianapolis Senior Center Fitness Center
708 E. Michigan St. **(M-5)**
263-6272
www.yourcenter.org

The fitness program uses exercise equipment and is tailored to individual needs under the guidance of a health educator. Open Mondays, Thursdays, and Fridays. No charge, but a $25 per month contribution is suggested.

Kelley/Myers Karate & Self Defense
940 Indiana Av. **(M-16)**
266-9276
www.kelleymyerskarate.com

The children's program is designed for kids age 3 to 12, after which the teen/adult programs click in, offering "a unique approach to self defense and exercise that benefits the body and the mind."

CHAPTER 9

Keeping a Car Downtown

Sunday mornings are great downtown. Compared to weekdays, you have the whole place to yourself. The parking lots are empty, the parking meters are asleep, the streets are still. You can shoot a cannon down Illinois Street and hit nothing more than a Saturday night whim.

Of course, you can't really shoot a cannon down Illinois Street—or Delaware, Alabama, New York, Capitol, or any other broad way. But downtown Indy still looks like an empty movie set on most Sunday mornings, a stage for your fantasies.

Monday mornings also are great downtown. The fantasies fade as the place awakens to a new week of opportunity and challenge. For many downtown residents, a routine everyday concern is finding a safe place to park the car or cars. This chapter discusses parking and car security, plus a bit of car philosophy.

Parking

The parking problem is very different for downtown residents compared to downtown commuters. If you commute downtown to work, shop, or have fun, finding a reasonably priced parking spot is fairly easy. In fact, compared to most other major U.S. downtowns, downtown Indy is very easy to enter and exit. We have broad main streets, synchronized traffic lights, and plenty of parking places—68,000, according to Indianapolis Downtown, Inc. The fastest way to check garage locations and rates is to go to the IDI website: www.indydt.com/parkingdatabase.html.

But if you live downtown, parking your car or cars 24-7 may be a different story. If you have more cars than you have garage or parking spaces and you must keep a vehicle on the street, you may be competing for parking space on weekdays with folks who drive to work in downtown Indy and park in front of your dwelling place rather than pay for parking space in a private lot. Some downtown neighborhood streets are protected from the freeloaders with official city postings restricting parking to neighborhood residents. Windshield stickers are issued to residents to identify their cars.

Parking at a Metered Spot

All is not lost, parking-wise, if the street outside your dwelling is lined with parking meters. Meters in downtown Indy are on duty Monday through Friday, starting at 7, 8, or 9 a.m. depending on the street, and quitting at 5 or 6 p.m. So if you take your vehicle elsewhere during those hours, you're home free.

Weekends are even better. You can park when the evening free hours begin on Friday and leave your car there until Monday morning without getting a ticket. But keep an eye on the clock—enforcement is vigorous.

Renting Space in a Parking Lot Downtown

The parking solution for some downtowners may be to rent a permanent parking spot in a downtown lot. The following table, compiled from information posted at the IDI website, shows parking facilities that are open 24 hours a day and offer monthly contracts. Some places have a waiting list and prices do change, so it's wise to confirm details. (And while you're doing that, reflect on parking costs in Indy compared to other places—like midtown Manhattan, NYC. Monthly parking space there is seldom below $250 for the least convenient lots but more like $600 to $1,000 a month near Fifth Avenue.)

Lot/Garage Name	Address	Telephone	Monthly Rate
Claypool Court	33 N. Capitol	632-9805	$100
National City Centre/Hyatt	5 S. Capitol	632-2893	$95
PanAm Plaza	240 S. Illinois	237-5790	$100
Adams Mark Garage	130 W. Market	972-0600	$130
Radisson Hotel	55 W. Ohio	635-2000	$120
Express Lot #319	319 E. Ohio	639-9825	$80
Capitol Commons	10 S. Capitol	951-0866	$100
Chatterbox Lot	435 Massachusetts	267-1400	$50
New Jersey & Vermont	418 E. Vermont	464-8100	$55
Express Lot #411	411 E. Ohio	639-9825	$60
Express Lot #401	401 E. Ohio	639-9825	$60
Alabama & Mass Av Lot	363 Massachusetts	632-2893	$75
Penn Park Lot	135 E. Market	633-6300	$110
North Senate	535 N. Senate	686-0486	$40
North Capitol	530 N. Capitol	686-0486	$40
Dorsa Lot	419 E. Ohio	638-5805	$50
Central 301 Lot	301 E. Washington	237-5790	$70
Penn Center Lot	440 N. Delaware	632-2893	$75
Penn & Vermont	407 N. Pennsylvania	632-2893	$75
Ober Lot	107 S. Pennsylvania	633-4003	$80

As of May 2004

Keeping Your Car Intact

Theft from vehicles is one of the most common crimes downtown, according to the Indianapolis Police Department (see Chapter 10 for downtown crime statistics). Considering the number of cars downtown everyday, odds are nobody will ever touch yours. But just to be safe, your best defense against a smashed window or pried door is to leave nothing of value within sight inside your car. If you drive an SUV, you may not have a handy place, like a trunk, to stow valuable stuff.

Servicing Your Car Downtown

You have all the service options downtown that you have in the suburbs—lubrication, tires, transmissions, body work, and the rest. You can also buy a car downtown. Check the numerous Directory listings under "Car."

Upscaling Your Life by Downscaling Your Fleet

You may have an opportunity when you move downtown to reduce your transportation budget. This doesn't work for everyone, but even if you have genuinely needed more than one car to serve your household needs while living in the suburbs, you may find because of your place of employment or the work status of household members that one car is all you need downtown. Much of what's appealing (and essential) downtown is within walking distance. For the moment, keeping more than one car downtown is not impossible or unreasonably expensive. But as the residential population of downtown Indy grows, the competition for parking space, and the cost, will only increase.

Getting to the Airport

Getting to and from Indianapolis International Airport is oh so easy when you live in downtown Indy. When our kids fly into town they call us on their cell phones as the plane touches down, and that's our cue to buzz out and pick them up, a 15-minute drive from our house. They're usually waiting at the curb.

But if you're the one who's flying, you have three choices:

◎ Drive, and park in a remote lot to keep your parking expense as low as possible.

◎ Call a taxi like Yellow (487-7777) and pay about $19 to $21 one way from the Monument Circle neighborhood. Or call a limo like Carey (241-7100) and pay $11 per person for shared-ride service.

◎ Take IndyGo bus No. 8, the Washington St. bus, from any bus stop on Ohio Street. One-way fare is $1.25, exact amount required (a dollar bill and a quarter coin will work). Buses depart every 30 minutes at :10 and :40, the ride takes 28 minutes, and you get off at the ground transportation terminal, just across the driveway from the airport entrance doors. The return trip leaves from the same place at :14 and :44. The No. 8 operates from 5 a.m. to 11:30 p.m. daily. If you are traveling light, IndyGo is a good option.

Calling the Cops–or Your City-County Council Rep

To report an accident, fire, serious illness, injury, or crime in progress that requires immediate response, call **9-1-1.**

But if your business with the police department, fire department, elected representative on the Indianapolis-Marion County City-County Council or other sector of local government is less urgent, let this chapter be your guide. The chapter contains:

◎ Crime statistics comparing downtown Indianapolis to north suburban Carmel, Indiana.

◎ The names and contact details for the three members of the City-County Council whose jurisdictions cover portions of downtown Indy. For when you have a complaint or suggestion, or just want to say "Nice job."

◎ Guidelines from the Indianapolis Historic Preservation Commission concerning home improvements and landscaping—if you live in an historic preservation district and must receive IHPC approval for certain kinds of work on the exterior of your house.

◎ A handy list of phone numbers covering various kinds of non-emergency assistance from local government agencies.

Staying Safe Downtown

Downtown Indianapolis is very safe, especially when you consider the number of people and vehicles downtown day and night. The crime statistics in this section provide ample evidence. When you take a close look at the numbers and consider the message they're sending you, it's easy to adopt habits that tend to keep you safe downtown.

According to the Indianapolis Police Department, the two largest kinds of crime downtown are assault ("a violent verbal or physical attack"—*Webster's II New College*), often associated with excessive celebrating; and theft from parked vehicles. The sensible response, IPD officers advise, is to steer clear of bar room brawls (gee, that was hard) and remember not to leave anything in plain sight when you park and lock your car in a public place. In other words, be cool. Remember that you're sharing downtown with lots of people, and a few of them may not be as mannerly as you are.

The following table shows the incidence of serious crime over a two-year period in the IPD Downtown District and, for comparison, north suburban Carmel, generally regarded as a very nice place to live.

	Downtown Indianapolis Pop. *123,742		Carmel, Indiana Pop. 57,000	
	2002	2003	2002	2003
Murder	0	1	0	0
Rape	9	12	5	3
Robbery	94	78	10	7
Assault	411	390	100	120
Burglary	146	157	80	115
Theft	1048	1064	566	612
Vehicle Theft	102	122	50	30
Totals	**1810**	**1824**	**811**	**887**

At first glance it may appear that Carmel is safer than downtown Indy, but that's not necessarily the case, as explained in a moment. Before the analysis, however, a few words about where these numbers come from. The crime stats are from the annual FBI reports prepared by the Indianapolis and Carmel police departments. The population figure for Carmel, 57,000, is the official city estimate in the spring of 2004.

The population figure for Indianapolis bears an asterisk because it's a combination of two numbers: the current estimate of downtown residents, 17,240; plus the number of people who work in downtown Indy, 106,502, both according to Indianapolis Downtown, Inc. Thus, a total for downtown of 123,742.

Actually, that's a conservative number—it doesn't account for the 1.7 million people who come to downtown Indy for conventions each year, or the 18.3 million (stats for the year 2000) who flock downtown for various other major attractions each year, according to numbers gathered by the Indianapolis Convention & Visitors Association. Some people may argue that daytime worker population and visitor population don't count in crime rates. But police officers disagree. Crime occurs where opportunity presents itself to criminals, and that's where people gather, as Captain John Bent of the IPD Downtown District will confirm. Capt. Bent notes that twenty-plus years ago, before downtown became a popular destination, two officers could take care of regular patrol. Today, a force of ten to fifteen are on regular assignment downtown.

But back to that difference in numbers of crimes between downtown Indy and Carmel. To compare the two places you have to convert the raw numbers to the same population basis, which is the standard FBI basis of "crimes per 100,000 population." The math is simple. Taking Carmel, for example, you divide the population, 57,000, by 100,000, with a result of 0.57. Then you divide each raw number in the crime report by the same 0.57. The procedure's identical for converting raw numbers of the downtown Indy report except that the divisor is 1.23. The results look like the following table.

	Downtown Indianapolis Pop. *123,742		Carmel, Indiana Pop. 57,000	
	2002	**2003**	**2002**	**2003**
Murder	0	1	0	0
Rape	7	10	9	5
Robbery	76	63	18	12
Assault	334	317	175	211
Burglary	119	128	140	202
Theft	852	865	993	1074
Vehicle Theft	83	99	88	53
Totals	**1471**	**1483**	**1423**	**1557**

As the table above demonstrates, downtown Indy is no more perilous a place, overall, than our well-mannered neighbor to the north. Just remember to keep your credit card under control and you'll do fine.

Contacting Your Council Rep

Because three districts of the Indianapolis/Marion County City-County Council converge downtown, figuring out who your Council representative is can be a little tricky. You have to know where you live with respect to the district boundary lines.

If you live south of Washington Street, including the south side of Washington Street, you are in the 19th District and your district representative is Dane Mahern, Democrat, reachable at 506-2707 or dmmahern@hotmail.com.

If you live north of Washington Street and west or south of the zigzag line formed by Michigan, New Jersey, North, Alabama, St. Clair, and Delaware streets (see zigzag sketch), you are in the 15th District and your district representative is Patrice Abduallah, Democrat, reachable at 262-8943 or Patrice4Council@yahoo.com.

If you live north or east of that zigzag line, you are in the 9th District and your district representative is Jackie Nytes, Democrat, reachable at 370-6184 or jackie@jackienytes.com.

The Council meets Mondays at 7 p.m. in the City-County Building **(M-24)**. To check the meeting schedule, go to www.indygov.org or type "Indianapolis City-County Council" in your search engine and you'll go straight to the Council home page.

Staying Out of Trouble with the Historians

If you buy a place downtown that's within the boundaries of an Historic Preservation District (check the neighborhoods map in Chapter 1) you have to follow a number of rules—"guidelines" is the softer word but the effect is the same—governing what you can do to the outside of your building, including landscaping, fencing, backyard pools, ornamental concrete geese, etc. The Indianapolis Historic Preservation Commission (type that name in your search engine and you'll get all the details) reviews and passes judgment on all plans for land use and modifications to existing buildings within the designated historic districts.

The overall objective is "to preserve the character and fabric of historically significant areas and structures for all present and future citizens of Marion County, Indiana." Given the pace of change in downtown Indy, that's a daunting task, but the IHPC generally gets high marks for both vigilance and fairness. Your part as a property owner is to cooperate. And it pays to do so: Real estate appreciates more rapidly when it's protected by design and zoning rules, the experts say.

The original big plan for each downtown Indy neighborhood was determined jointly by IHPC and neighborhood residents, so the broad scope of guidelines varies a bit from place to place. But in general they follow standards of the U.S. Secretary of the Interior for historic preservation projects nationwide. Here is what those 10 standards say, as presented at the IHPC website:

1. A property shall be used for its historic purpose or be placed in a new use that requires minimal change to the defining characteristics of the building and its site and environment.

2. The historic character of a property shall be retained and preserved. The removal of historic material or alteration of features and spaces that characterize a property shall be avoided.

3. Each property shall be recognized as a physical record of its time, place, and use. Changes that create a false sense of historical development, such as adding conjectural features or architectural elements from other buildings, shall not be undertaken.

4. Most properties change over time; those changes that have acquired historic significance in their own right shall be retained and preserved.

5. Distinctive stylistic features or examples of skilled craftsmanship which characterize a building, structure, or site, should be treated with sensitivity.

6. Deteriorated historic features shall be repaired rather than replaced. Where the severity of deterioration requires replacement of a distinctive feature, the new feature shall match the old in design, color, texture, and other visual qualities and, where possible, materials. Replacement of missing features shall be substantiated by documentary, physical, or pictorial evidence.

7. Chemical or physical treatments, such as sandblasting, that cause damage to historic materials shall not be used. The surface cleaning of structures, if appropriate, shall be undertaken using the gentlest means possible.

8. Significant archeological resources affected by a project shall be protected and preserved. If such resources must be disturbed, mitigation measures shall be undertaken.

9. New additions, exterior alterations, or related new construction shall not destroy historic materials that characterize the property. The new work shall be differentiated from the old and shall be compatible with the massing, size, scale, and architectural features to protect the historic integrity of the property and its environment.

10. New additions and adjacent or related new construction shall be undertaken in such a manner that if removed in the future, the essential form and integrity of the historic property and its environment would be unimpaired.

For full particulars, call the IHPC office, 317-327-4409, or go to the website: www.indygov.org/histpres.

Dialing for Details or Service

Here's a handy reference list of telephone numbers covering a variety of everyday needs:

IPD Downtown District 327-6500
Abandoned vehicles 327-4622
Accident reports, IPD. 327-3408
Citizens' complaints 327-3440
Dead animal pickup. 327-4622
Indianapolis Public School Police 226-4669
Mayor's Action Center. 327-4622
Parks Department 327-0000
Street or signal repair 327-4622

Downtown Directory

This part of the book is your guide to everything you can find at street level in downtown Indy. To understand what's included, imagine that you start at the northeast corner of the Northeast Quadrant (Chapter 1 explains the quadrants) and walk around every downtown block until you reach the southwest corner of the Southwest Quadrant. On your Palm Pilot or clipboard you record everything that you pass by—every store, every apartment building and condo development, every restaurant, every museum, factory, school, office building, park, monument, performance hall, mailbox, Fedex drop site—everything. Then you arrange all this data alphabetically so you can refer to it quickly, like a classified telephone book. Finally, to make it easy to get to places listed in the directory, you draw maps—Chapter 12 contains the maps—and you key each directory listing to a map with an **M** number (like **M-25,** the block where Circle Centre appears). That's how the directory works.

The directory has a few limitations that you should understand. Because it's primarily a *street-level* record of downtown features useful to downtown residents, meaning primarily a guide to retail stores and consumer services, it includes only what's visible from the street. So, with only a few exceptions, you won't find the inside, upper-floor tenants of buildings accounted for here. The main exceptions are stores and services located inside Circle Centre, all listed in Chapter 3; and City Market, all listed in this directory.

One other thing the directory doesn't do is connect to topics covered in the chapters, like a conventional book index. But you can use the table of contents for that purpose. The chapters are fairly short and full of subheadings for easy skimming.

Advertising Agencies

Beltrame, Leffler Advertising, 716 Massachusetts Av., 916-9930, **M-6**
Bradley & Montgomery Advertising, 942 Ft. Wayne Av., 423-1745, **M-3**
Clear Channel Outdoor, 511 Madison Av., 634-1900, **M-32**
Hirons & Company, 135 S. Illinois St., 977-2206, **M-25**
The Promotion Company, Inc., 804 N. Delaware St., 236-6515, **M-4**
Roman Brand Group (formerly Bates USA), 117 E. Washington St., 686-7800, **M-24**
Young & Laramore, 310 E. Vermont St., 264-8000, **M-7**

Airborne Express Drop Boxes

Indiana Av. outside Gregory & Appel Insurance, 520 Indiana Av., 6 p.m. M-F, **M-19**
111 Monument Circle at garage level of Bank One Bldg., 7 p.m. M-F, **M-20**
Virginia & Washington Sts., in Jefferson Plaza Bldg., 5:30 p.m. M-F, **M-24**

Apartment Buildings

Alameda, The, 37 W. St. Clair St., 722-7115, **M-17**
Apollo-Aurora Apartments, 11th St. between Alabama & New Jersey, 684-7300, **M-3**
Argyle Apartments, 615 N. East St., 635-4200, **M-6**
B&B Apt., 522 E. Fletcher Av., **M-22**
Block, The, 50 N. Illinois St., 238-0100, **M-21**
Buschmann Grain Lofts, 970 Ft. Wayne Av., 635-8282, **M-3**
Calvin Fletcher Apartments, 520 Virginia Av., 786-0723, **M-30**
Canal Overlook Apartments, 430 Indiana Av., 634-6090, **M-19**
Canal Square Apartments, 359 N. West St., 631-7030, **M-19**
Cathcart Apartments, cnr Pennsylvania St. & 9th St., 684-7300, **M-4**
Chatham Manor, 708 11th St., **M-1**
Christian Place Apartments, Alabama St. & 9th St., 786-0723, **M-4**
Clifford, The, 709 Park Av., **M-6**
Colonial Apartments, 402 N. Delaware St., 636-7082, **M-8**
Continental Towers, The, 410 N. Meridian St., 972-4100, **M-17**
Davlan Court, 430 Massachusetts Av., 464-2435, **M-7**
Delaware Court Apartments, Delaware St. at 10th St., 354-9000, **M-4**
Devonshire Apartments, 412 N. Alabama St., 924-6256, **M-8**
Fletcher Place Apartments, 641 Stevens St., 753-2618, **M-30**
Garden Arch Apartments, St. Clair St. & East St., 684-7300, **M-7**

Gardenbrook Circle, Fayette & St. Clair Sts., **M-15**
Gardengate Place, Canal Walk between 9th & 10th Sts., **M-15**
Gardens, The, of Canal Court, Canal View, 636-2126, **M-15 & M-19**
Goodwin Plaza Apartments, 601 W. St. Clair St., 636-7218, **M-16**
Grace Manor Apartments, 234 E. 9th St., 955-0987, **M-4**
Harness Factory Lofts, The, 30 E. Georgia St., 632-2770, **M-25**
Historic Fletcher Place Apartments & Townhomes, Virginia Av. at Stevens St.,
       923-9036, **M-30**
Indiana Avenue Apartments, 825 Indiana Av., 423-2292, **M-16**
IUPUI Student Apartments, E of White River between New York & Michigan Sts., **M-29**
Janus Lofts, 255 S. McCrea St., 464-8254, **M-25**
Laco Towne Club Apartments, 842 N. Capitol Av., 923-4357, **M-14**
Lockefield Gardens, bounded by Indiana Av., Blake & Walnut Sts., adjacent to
       IUPUI, 631-2922, **M-16**
Lockerbie Apartments, 402 E. New York St., 636-7682, **M-11**
Lockerbie Court, 402 N. New Jersey St., 634-5555, **M-7**
Lockerbie Flats, 619 E. Vermont Pl., **M-10**
Lodge Apartments, Pennsylvania St. N of St. Clair St., 427-0927, **M-4**
Martens Apartments, 315 N. Senate Av., 955-8790, **M-18**
May-Leeno Apartments, 416 E. Vermont St., **M-7**
McKay Apartments, The, Pennsylvania St. N of Ft. Wayne Av., 488-8800, **M-8**
Plaza, The, NW cnr., Pennsylvania & 9th Sts., 634-5555, **M-13**
Pennsylvania, The, 919 N. Pennsylvania St., 684-7300, **M-4**
Renaissance Tower, 230 E. 9th St., 261-1652, **M-4**
Richelieu Apartments, 610 N. East St., 686-7212, **M-7**
Riley Towers 1, 542 N. Alabama St., 635-3300, **M-8**
Riley Towers 2, 600 N. Alabama St., 635-3300, **M-8**
Riley Towers 3, 700 N. Alabama St., 635-3300, **M-8**
Senate Manor Apartments, 545 & 548 N. Senate Av., 901-3715, **M-18**
Sencord Flats & Townhomes, 550 E. Fletcher Av., 972-1448, **M-23**
Senior Apartments, 960 N. Pennsylvania St., 464-2435, **M-13**
Stewart House, 212 E. 10th St., 443-5554, **M-4**
Turnverein, 902 N. Meridian St., 684-7496, **M-13**
Van Rooy Properties, 1030-1050 & 1112 N. College Av., **M-2**
Van Rooy Properties, 658 E. 11th St., **M-2**
Van Rooy Properties Management Office, 1030 N. College Av., 684-7300, **M-2**
Walnut St. at Cleveland St., Monument Management Corp., 464-2435, **M-7**
Wilson, The, 643 Ft. Wayne Av., **M-8**
Wyndham, The, 1040 N. Delaware St., 632-2912, **M-4**
Zender Apartments, 670 E. 11th St., 488-8800, **M-2**
Zender Apartments, Michigan St. between Delaware & Alabama Sts., 488-8800, **M-8**

Architects

Artekna, 321 E. New York St., 955-5090, **M-11**
Axis Architecture & Interiors, 618 E. Market St., 264-8162, **M-10**
Charles M. Brown, Inc., 531 W. 11th St., 262-8444, **M-16**
Entheos Architects, 623 N. East St., 951-9590, **M-6**
Hellmuth, Obata & Kassabaum, 107 S. Pennsylvania St., 634-7961, **M-24**
InterDesign, 141 E. Ohio St., 263-9655, **M-12A**
Ratio Architects, 107 S. Pennsylvania St., 633-4040, **M-24**
Schmidt Associates, 320 E. Vermont St., 263-6226, **M-7**

Art Dealers & Galleries

Boca Loca Beads & Art Glass Studio, 872 Massachusetts Av., 423-BEAD, **M-1**
Dean Johnson Design, Inc., 646 Massachusetts Av., 634-8020, **M-6**
Domont Art Gallery, 545 S. East St., 685-9634, **M-30**
Ebony Art Images, 50 S. Meridian St., 632-3838, **M-25**
Frame Shop, The, 617 Massachusetts Av., 822-8455, **M-6**
Kuaba Gallery, 876 Massachusetts Av., 955-8405, **M-1**
McFee Gallery of Modern Art, 874 Massachusetts Av., 822-5922, **M-1**
Perfect Gift, City Market, 783-2602, **M-12**
Red Dot Fine Art Glass Gallery, 882 Massachusetts Av., **M-1**
Ruschman Art Gallery, 948 N. Alabama St., 634-3114, **M-4**

Associations

American College of Sports Medicine, 401 W. Michigan St., 637-9200, **M-19**
American Legion, The, 700 N. Pennsylvania St., 630-1200, **M-17**
Indiana Bar Foundation, 230 E. Ohio St., 269-2415, **M-12**
Indiana Dental Association, 401 W. Michigan St., 634-2610, **M-19**
Indiana Farm Bureau Incorporated, 225 S. East St., 692-7851, **M-23**
Indiana Pharmacists Alliance, 729 N. Pennsylvania St., 634-4968, **M-8**
Indianapolis Medical Society, 631 E. New York St., 639-3406, **M-10**
Indianapolis Urban League, 777 Indiana Av., 639-9404, **M-16**
National Collegiate Athletic Association (NCAA), 750 W. Washington St.,
    916-4255, **M-27**
National Federation of State High School Associates, 750 W. Washington St.,
    972-6000, **M-27**
Phi Kappa Psi Fraternity National Headquarters, 510 Lockerbie St., 632-1852, **M-10**
Sigma Theta Tau Int'l & Center for Nursing Scholarship, 550 W. North St.,
    634-8171, **M-16**

ATMs ($)

Bank One, 101 Monument Circle, **M-20**
Fifth Third Bank, 251 N. Illinois St., 383-2300, **M-20**
Fifth Third Bank, SE cnr Ohio & East Sts., **M-10**
Fifth Third Bank, NW cnr Monument Circle & Market St., **M-20**
Firefighters Credit Union, 501 N. New Jersey St., **M-7**

First Indiana Bank, 135 N. Pennsylvania St., 269-1200, **M-12A**
Flagstar Bank, 2 N. Meridian St., 634-0916, **M-20**
Forum Credit Union, 120 Monument Circle, 558-6000, **M-20**
Huntington Banks, 251 N. Illinois St., 237-2575, **M-20**
Irwin Union Bank, 300 N. Meridian St., 888-879-5900, **M-20**
IUPUI School of Liberal Arts, Bank One, 425 University Blvd., **M-27**
IUPUI Union Building, Star, 620 Union Dr., **M-28**
IUPUI, Wishard Blvd. at Barnhill Dr., Bank One, **M-28**
Keybank, 10 W. Market St., 464-8000, **M-20**
Landmark Savings Bank, 54 Monument Circle, 633-0900, **M-20**
National Bank of Indianapolis, City Market, **M-12**
National Bank of Indianapolis, 107 N. Pennsylvania St., 261-9000, **M-12A**
National City Bank, 155 E. Market St., 756-5010, **M-24**
National City Bank, 101 W. Washington St., 267-7900, **M-26**
Old National Bank, 101 W. Ohio St., 693-2552, **M-21**
Teachers Credit Union, 1 N. Capitol Av., 624-6900, **M-21**
Union Federal Bank, 45 N. Pennsylvania St., 269-4735, **M-24**
Union Planters Bank, Main Office, Ohio St. between Pennsylvania & Delaware Sts.,
    221-6000, **M-12**
Union Planters Bank – Riley Center, 555 N. Delaware St., 221-6850, **M-8**
University Place Hotel & Conference Center, 850 W. Michigan St., **M-28**

Attorneys

Baker & Daniels, 300 N. Meridian St., 237-3000, **M-20**
Baker Pittman & Page, 333 E. Ohio St., 686-1900, **M-11**
Barnes & Thornburg, 11 S. Meridian St., 236-1313, **M-25**
Bingham McHale LLP, 10 W. Market St., 635-8900, **M-20**
Brooks, Koch & Sorg, 615 Russell Av., 822-3700, **M-32**
Brown, Tompkins & Lory, 608 E. Market St., 631-6866, **M-10**
Cline, Farrell, Christie, Lee & Caress, 951 N. Delaware St., 488-5500, **M-4**
Forbes, Schmitt & Kotzan, 131 E. Ohio St., 631-3100, **M-12A**
Charles D. Hankey Law Office, 434 E. New York St., 634-8565, **M-11**
Jones & Jones, 717 S. East St., 639-2243, **M-30**
Haskin Lauter & LaRue, 255 N. Alabama St., 955-9500, **M-11**
Thomas F. Hastings, 323 N. Delaware St., 685-2320, **M-12**
Hendren Law Office, New York St. between New Jersey & East Sts., 685-2525, **M-11**
Hensley & Associates, 426 E. New York St., 472-3333, **M-11**
Katz & Korin, 340 N. Senate Av., 464-1100, **M-19**
Linder & Hollowell, 728 S. Meridian St., 637-3170, **M-32**
McClure McClure & Davis, 235 N. Delaware St., 221-0800, **M-12**
Mike Norris Law Office, 22 E. Washington St., 266-8888, **M-20**
Mitchell Hurst Jacobs & Dick, 152 E. Washington St., 636-0808, **M-24**
Pardieck, Gill & Vargo, 244 N. College Av., 639-3315, **M-10**
Schnorr, Maier, & Olvey, 144 N. Delaware St., 264-3636, **M-12A**
White & Johnson, Lawyers, 302 N. East St., 638-1468, **M-11**

Young & Young, 128 N. Delaware St., 639-5161, **M-12A**
Mark S. Zuckerberg, P.C., 333 N. Pennsylvania St., 687-0000, **M-12**

Bagels
Einstein Bros. Bagels, 47 S. Illinois St., 917-9888, **M-25**

Bail Bonds
AAA Bail Bonds, Inc., 155 N. Alabama St., 635-6570, **M-11**
Bail Bonds Advantage, 114 N. Delaware St., 972-4776, **M-12A**
Byron's No Limit Bail Bonds, Inc., 124 N. Delaware St., 635-2003, **M-12A**
Cheryl Fortune Bail Bonds, 44 Virginia Av., 634-2000, **M-24**
City Bonding, Delaware St. opposite City-County Bldg., 236-1600, **M-24**
Indiana Bail Bonds, 850 N. Meridian St., 972-8888, **M-13**
Marsh Bail Bonds, 101 S. Alabama St., 632-4357, **M-24**
Roach Bail Bonds, 36 N. Delaware St., 822-3552, **M-24**
State Bail Bonding, 22 N. Delaware St., 236-6560, **M-24**
Wooden Bail Bonds, 151 E. Market St., 955-2663, **M-24**

Banks & Credit Unions
Bank One, 101 Monument Circle, 321-7020, **M-20**
Fifth Third Bank, 251 N. Illinois St., 383-2300, **M-20**
Fifth Third Bank, SE cnr Ohio & East Sts., **M-10**
Fifth Third Bank, NW cnr Monument Circle & Market St., **M-20**
First Indiana Bank, 135 N. Pennsylvania St., 269-1200, **M-12A**
Flagstar Bank, 2 N. Meridian St., 634-0916, **M-20**
Forum Credit Union, 120 Monument Circle, 558-6000, **M-20**
Huntington Banks, 251 N. Illinois St., 237-2575, **M-20**
Irwin Union Bank, 300 N. Meridian St., 888-879-5900, **M-20**
Keybank, 10 W. Market St., 464-8000, **M-20**
Landmark Savings Bank, 54 Monument Circle, 633-0900, **M-20**
National Bank of Indianapolis, 107 N. Pennsylvania St., 261-9000, **M-12A**
National City Bank, 155 E. Market St., 756-5010, **M-24**
National City Bank, 101 W. Washington St., 267-7900, **M-26**
Old National Bank, 101 W. Ohio St., 693-2552, **M-21**
Teachers Credit Union, 1 N. Capitol Av., 624-6900, **M-21**
Union Federal Bank, 45 N. Pennsylvania St., 269-4735, **M-24**
Union Planters Bank, Main Office, Ohio St. between Pennsylvania & Delaware Sts.,
    221-6000, **M-12**
Union Planters Bank – Riley Center, 555 N. Delaware St., 221-6850, **M-8**

Barber Shops
Downtown Barber & Beauty Salon, 115 E. Vermont St., 631-2211, **M-12**
The Barber/The Hairdresser, 659 Virginia Av., 231-9028, **M-30**

Beauty Salons

The Barber/The Hairdresser, 659 Virginia Av., 231-9028, **M-30**
Complexions Day Spa, 735 Massachusetts Av., 423-9000, **M-6**
Fixx Hair Studio, 308 E. New York St., 229-2935, **M-11**
Gazebo, 427 Massachusetts Av., 262-9666, **M-7**
Legends Salon, 845 Massachusetts Av., 631-2155, **M-1**
Mass Appeal, 700 Massachusetts Av., 635-4737, **M-6**
New Order Hair Design & Day Spa, 610 Massachusetts Av., 266-8787, **M-6**
Number Sixteen Delaware, 14 N. Delaware St., 237-0710, **M-24**
Rene's, 114 E. 9th St., 266-0598, **M-4**
Sirens, 607 Massachusetts Av., 262-9650, **M-6**
Space 934 Hair Salon, 934 Ft. Wayne Av., 916-5890, **M-3**
Studio 2000 Salon & Day Spa, 55 Monument Circle, 687-0010, **M-20**
Textures Studio Salon, 50 S. Meridian St., Suite 104, 917-9737, **M-25**
Walker Building Beauty Salon, 619 Indiana Av., 631-0525, **M-16**
Xcentrix Style Studio, 247 E. 11th St., 687-8953, **M-4**

Beauty Supplies

Jenny's Boutique, 36 E. Washington St., 635-1255, **M-20**

Bed & Breakfasts

Nestle Inn, 637 N. East St., 610-5200, **M-6**

Bike Rentals

The Bike Shop, 922 Massachusetts Av., 687-8768, **M-1**
Wheel Fun Bike Rentals, White River State Park, 767-5072, **M-27**

Blood Banks

Indianapolis Blood Plasma, Inc., 502 N. Capitol Av., 637-3294, **M-18**

Boat Rentals

Wheel Fun Boat Rentals, Ohio St. Basin of Canal Walk, 767-5072, **M-22**

Bookstores

Architectural Center Bookstore, 47 S. Pennsylvania St. (2nd Floor), 634-3871, **M-24**
Borders Books, Music & Café, 11 S. Meridian St., 972-8595, **M-25**
Cavanaugh Bookstore, IUPUI, 425 University Blvd., 278-2665, **M-27**
Doubleday Book Shop, Circle Centre, 632-4910, **M-25**
Out Word Bound Bookstore, 625 N. East St., 951-9100, **M-6**
Indy's College Bookstore, 601 W. 11th St., 631-2665, **M-16**
IU Medical/Law Bookstore, Union Building, 620 Union Dr., 274-7167, **M-28**
X-pression Bookstore & Gallery, 970 Ft. Wayne Av., 264-1866, **M-3**

Building Materials

Affordable Building Supplies, LLC, 212 W. McCarty St., 636-0445, **M-33**

Jobsite Supply, 624 S. Missouri St., 684-7474, 383-0332, **M-33**

Buildings (Named)

Algonquin, 225 N. Delaware St., **M-12**

Amalgamated Auditorium, 9th St. between Capitol Av. & Muskingum St., **M-14**

Ambassador Hotel, SW cnr. Pennsylvania & 9th Sts., **M-13**

American Building, SE cnr Pennsylvania & Vermont Sts., **M-12**

Argyle, The, NE cnr East St. & Massachusetts Av., **M-6**

AUL Tower, NW cnr Ohio & Illinois Sts., **M-21**

Bank One Center, 101-111 Monument Circle, **M-20**

Barrister Building, The, 155 E. Market St., **M-24**

Barton House, NE cnr Michigan & Delaware Sts., **M-8**

Birch Bayh Federal Building & United States Court House, 46 E. Ohio St., **M-20**

Blacherne, 402 N. Meridian St., **M-17**

Block Building, William H., 50 N. Illinois St., 635-7401, **M-21**

Brougher Building, The, Meridian St. S of Henry St., **M-32**

Brougher International Building, 407 Fulton St., **M-5**

Calvin Fletcher School, 520 Virginia Av., **M-30**

Capital Center, 251 N. Illinois St., 237-2800, **M-20**

Edward T. Carlson Hall, 849 S. Meridian St., **M-32**

Center Township Trustee, 863 Massachusetts Av., 633-3610, **M-1**

Century Building, 36 S. Pennsylvania St., **M-25**

Chamber of Commerce, 320 N. Meridian St., **M-20**

Cigna Health Care, 429 N. Pennsylvania St., **M-8**

Circle Tower, 55 Monument Circle, 634-1700, **M-20**

Clemens Vonnegut School (Brougher International Building), 407 Fulton St., **M-5**

Coca-Cola Bottling Co., Bellfontaine Av., **M-1**

Cohen Technology Center, Robert H., 715 N. Senate Av., **M-14**

Commercial Building, The, 207-9 N. Delaware St., **M-12**

Consolidated Building, 115 N. Pennsylvania St., **M-12A**

Louis G. Deschler, 135 S. Illinois St., **M-25**

Emelie, 340-42 N. Senate Av., **M-19**

Emmis Communications, 40 Monument Circle, **M-20**

English Foundation Building, 615 N. Alabama St., **M-7**

Fifth Third Bank, 251 N. Illinois St., **M-20**

54 Monument Circle, **M-20**

543 E. Market Professional Building, **M-23**

500 Building, NE cnr Ohio St. & East St., **M-10**

Firefighters Hall, 748 Massachusetts Av., **M-6**

Fire Headquarters, SE cnr New York & Alabama Sts., **M-11**

Fire Station No. 12, NW cnr New Jersey & South Sts., **M-24**

Gateway Plaza, 950 N. Meridian St., 573-6060, **M-13**

Guaranty Building, 10 N. Meridian St., **M-20**

Harrison Building, 143 W. Market St., 635-6218, **M-21**
Harlan Hoffman House, 440 N. East St., **M-7**
Haugh, The, 127 E. Michigan St., **M-8**
Heier, The, 10 S. New Jersey St., **M-24**
Illinois Building, 17 W. Market St., **M-20**
Indiana Bar Center, 230 E. Ohio St., **M-12**
Indiana Business Journal, 41 E. Washington St., **M-25**
Indiana Government Center North, 100 N. Senate Av., **M-22**
Indiana Government Center South, 302-402 W. Washington St., **M-22**
Indiana Rotary Convalescent Home, 702 West Dr., **M-28**
Indiana State Library & Historical Building, 140 N. Senate Av., **M-22**
Indianapolis City Market, 222 E. Market St., 634-9266, **M-12**
ISTA Center, 150 W. Market St., 633-6300, **M-21**
Jefferson Plaza, 1 Virginia Av., **M-24**
Landmark Center, 1099 N. Meridian St., 630-3626, **M-13**
Link, 401 N. Illinois St., **M-17**
Robert W. Long Hospital, 1110 Medical Dr., **M-28**
Madame C. J. Walker Building, 617 Indiana Av., **M-16**
Majestic Building, 47 S. Pennsylvania St., **M-24**
Market Square Center, 151 N. Delaware St., 236-2000, **M-12**
Market Tower, 10 W. Market St., 464-8213, **M-20**
Marott Center, 342 Massachusetts Av., **M-12**
Mayer Chapel & Neighborhood House, 448 W. Norwood St., **M-33**
Mid-States Engineering, NW cnr New Jersey & New York Sts., **M-11**
Minton Capehart Federal Building, 575 N. Pennsylvania St., **M-8**
MNA, NW cnr New York & New Jersey Sts., **M-11**
Morrison Opera Place, 47-49 S. Meridian St., **M-25**
Murray Building, 30 E. Georgia St., **M-25**
National City Center, 101 W. Washington St., **M-26**
Old National, 101 W. Ohio St., **M-21**
Old Trails Building, 309 W. Washington St., **M-22**
One America, Senate Av. between North & Walnut Sts., **M-18**
One North Capitol, NE cnr Capitol Av. & Washington St., 808-6000, **M-21**
135 N. Pennsylvania Building, **M-12A**
136 E. Market Street, **M-12A**
Pan American Plaza, 201 S. Capitol Av., 237-5794, **M-26**
Publix Theatre, 140 W. Washington St., **M-21**
Radio One, 21 E. St. Joseph St., 266-9600, **M-13**
Safeco, 500 N. Meridian St., **M-17**
Service Supply Co., 603 E. Washington St., 472-1800, **M-23**
Shelton, The, 825 Delaware St., **M-4**
Standard Oil Company, 802 E. Lord St., **M-23**
Stutz Building, 1060 N. Capitol Av., 488-7373, **M-14**
Thomas Jefferson #7, 748 E. Bates St., **M-23**
300 N. Meridian St., NW cnr of Meridian and New York Sts., **M-20**

Trowel Trades Building, 620 N. East St., 631-3600, **M-7**

21 N. Pennsylvania St., **M-24**

Union Federal Building, 45 N. Pennsylvania St., 636-7609, **M-24**

Vienna, The, NE cnr New York & Alabama Sts., **M-11**

Walker Plaza, 719 Indiana Av., **M-16**

Wulsin, 222 E. Ohio St., **M-12**

Business-to-Business Services & Supplies

R. B. Annis Co., 1101 N. Delaware St., 637-9282, **M-4**

AT&T AWS, 710 Kentucky Av., **M-34**

AT&T Company, 112 W. North St., 383-3000, **M-18**

Bar Steel Service Center, 627 N. College Av., 684-8272, **M-5**

BE, Inc., 1060 N. Capitol Av., 974-1295, **M-14**

Buyers Paper & Specialty Co., Inc., 510 W. Merrill St., 684-7500, **M-34**

Carey Digital, 635 E. Market St., 637-9060, **M-23**

Central Restaurant Products, 1010 Central Av., 634-2550, **M-3**

Central Stainless Equipment, Inc., 943 S. Meridian St., 632-5365, **M-32**

Certified Welding Co., 227 W. McCarty St., 637-2912, **M-33**

Christie Machine Works, Inc., 425 W. McCarty St., 638-8840, **M-33**

Crescent Oil Co., Inc., 514 W. Wyoming St., 634-1415, **M-34**

Custom Fabricating Inc., 701 Kentucky Av., 635-1177, **M-34**

DCG, 644 E. Washington St., 635-7827, **M-23**

Design Plus, 702 N. Illinois St., **M-14**

Design-Aire Consultants, 220 N. College Av., 464-9090, **M-10**

Diamond Chain Co., Inc., 402 Kentucky Av., 638-6431, **M-34**

R. E. Dimond & Associates, Inc., Consulting Engineers, 732 N. Capitol Av., 634-4672, **M-14**

Dixon Vending, Inc., 202 N. College Av., 631-9318, **M-10**

Dominion Telecom, 800 Oliver Av., 888-472-0751, **M-34**

Dorfman Property Management, 827 N. Capitol Av., 634-6780, **M-14**

Duncan Supply Co., Inc., 910 N. Illinois St. & 905 N. Capitol Av., 634-1335, **M-14**

Emmis Communications Corp., 40 Monument Circle, 266-0100, **M-20**

Engine Parts Warehouse, Inc., 155 N. College Av., 917-8020, **M-9**

Enzo & Associates, 29 E. McCarty St., 638-0357, **M-32**

Eskye.com Inc., 733 S. West St., 632-3870, **M-33**

ETE Wholesale Transmission & Supply, 825 N. Capitol Av., 635-0111, **M-14**

B. H. Gardner Co., Bakery Supplies, 350 W. St. Clair St., 634-4431, **M-15**

Genuity Telecom, 175 N. College Av., 633-4834, **M-9**

Gill Saw Service, 10 W. McCarty St., 631-2375, **M-32**

Global Crossing, 700 W. Henry St., **M-34**

Handschy Industries, 528 Fulton St., 636-5565, **M-5**

Heavyweights, The, 1010 N. Capitol Av., 684-7777, **M-14**

Hebrew National Kosher Foods, 602 W. Ray St., 637-5093, **M-34**

Hoosier Mailing Equipment, 971 N. Delaware St., 632-6007, **M-4**

N. K. Hurst Co., 230 W. McCarty St., 631-7750, 634-6425, **M-33**

Impact Group, Inc., 501 Virginia Av., 636-7387, **M-30**
Indiana Fan & Fabrication, 427 S. Alabama St., 634-7165, **M-31**
Indianapolis Welding Co., 425 W. McCarty St., 638-8840, **M-33**
Indianapolis Welding Supply, Inc., 315 W. McCarty St., 632-2446, **M-33**
Keramida Environmental, Inc., 330 N. College Av., 685-6600, **M-10**
Kerr Refrigeration Appliance Service, 130 S. Davidson St., 637-6690, **M-23**
Lawler Manufacturing, Inc., 600 E. Ohio St., 261-1212, **M-10**
Bill Lawrence Co., Inc., 221 N. College Av., 632-0363, **M-9**
Level 3 Communications, 733 W. Henry St., **M-34**
Loomis Fargo & Co., 122 N. College Av., 632-3421, **M-10**
Albert G. Maas Co., Janitorial Supplies, 25 E. McCarty St., 632-8315, **M-32**
M.A.I.L. of Indy, Inc., 719 Virginia Av., 631-4172, **M-30**
Magnetech Industrial Services, Inc., 551 W. Merrill St., 266-1659, **M-34**
Marbaugh Reprographics & Supply, 801 N. Capitol Av., 631-1000, **M-14**
Matrix Imaging, 118 W. North St., 635-4756, **M-18**
MCI, 720 W. Henry St., **M-34**
Mitchell & Scott Machine Co., College St. & North St., **M-5**
Modern Photo Offset Supply, Inc., 536 E. Market St., 634-5500, **M-10**
National Wine & Spirits Co., 733 S. West St., 636-6092, **M-33**
Nemec Heating & Supply Co., 614 E. Ohio St., 635-7673, **M-10**
Norwood Promotional Products, 10 W. Market St., 275-2500, **M-20**
Omega Communications, Inc., 29 E. Maryland St., 264-4010, **M-25**
Park Supply, 915 S. Meridian St., **M-32**
PEN Property Employment Network, 40 Virginia Av., 974-0669, **M-24**
Pipe Shop, 819 N. Senate Av., **M-14**
Progress Laundry & Supply, Inc., 333 N. College St., 636-6588, **M-9**
Ray & Mascari, Inc., 324 S. New Jersey St., 637-0234, **M-24**
Recordspro.Net, 212 W. 10th St., 916-1880, **M-14**
Reel Pipe & Valve Co., 914 N. Senate Av., 634-8421, **M-15**
RJE Business Interiors, 621 E. Ohio St., 293-4051, **M-10**
Sapheo, 212 W. 10th St., 632-8866, **M-14**
Scherer Industrial Group, Inc., 940 S. West St., 231-2363, **M-34**
Scherer Industrial Group, Inc., 220 W. McCarty St., **M-33**
Shirley Engraving Co., 460 Virginia Av., 634-4084, **M-30**
Sonar Studios, Inc., 1060 N. Capitol Av., 972-4210, **M-14**
Standard Die Supply, 927 S. Pennsylvania St., 236-6200, **M-32**
Superior Distributing Co., Inc., 918 Ft. Wayne Av., 633-0555, **M-3**
Sutton-Garten Co. Welding Supplies, 901 N. Senate Av., 264-3236, **M-14**
Taylor & Blackburn Battery Warehouse, Inc., 918 S. Senate Av., 236-6288, **M-33**
Three-Sixty Group, a Cranfill Company, 36 S. Pennsylvania St., **M-25**
Triumph Communications, 631 E. New York St., 681-0556, **M-10**
Tway Company, Inc., 602 N. Park Av., 636-2591, **M-6**
Universal Supply, Inc., 104 S. College Av., 687-6767, **M-23**
University Loft Company, 433 E. Washington St., 631-5433, **M-24**
Visual Sign Co., 401 S. Alabama St., 632-7008, **M-31**

West Roofing & Building Materials, 602 W. McCarty St., 634-9031, **M-34**
Western Newspaper Publishing, Inc., 537 E. Ohio St., 636-4122, **M-10**
York Heating & Cooling Distributor, 910 N. Illinois St., 264-7785, **M-14**
Young and Sons, Inc., 412 W. McCarty St., 263-0960, **M-33**
Zoll Brothers/Zesco Products, 640 N. Capitol Av., 269-9300, **M-18**

Bus Lines
Greyhound Bus Lines, 350 S. Illinois St., 267-3071, 800-231-2222, **M-26**
IndyGo Public Transportation, 635-3344
IndyGo Downtown Shuttle, 635-3344

Cafeterias
Gabriel's Cafeteria, 320 N. Meridian St., 635-0132, **M-20**
Indiana Government Center, North & South buildings, **M-22**
Sahm's at The Plaza, 135 N. Pennsylvania St., 637-2850, **M-12A**
Shapiro's Delicatessen Cafeteria, 808 S. Meridian St., 631-4041, **M-32**

Camera Dealers
Cord Camera, 317 N. Delaware St., 972-4169, **M-12**
Roberts Distributors, 255 S. Meridian St., 636-5544, **M-25**

Candy Stores
Rocky Mountain Chocolate Factory, 28 Monument Circle, 687-1322, **M-20**
South Bend Chocolate Company Café, The, 30 Monument Circle, 951-4816, **M-20**
See also Circle Center listings in Chapter 3

Car Body Repairing & Painting
Church Brothers Collision Repair, 135 W. McCarty St., 262-5159, **M-32**

Car Parts
Harms Auto Supply, 622 E. Market St., 632-7447, **M-10**
Finishmaster Automotive Paint Stores, 923 N. Meridian St., 634-2466, **M-13**
Lincoln Auto Parts Co., 901 N. Capitol Av., 636-3484, **M-14**
NAPA Auto Parts, 415 W. McCarty St., 634-3524, **M-33**
Waymire's Trailer Towing Systems, 820 Chadwick St., 634-4824, **M-33**

Car Rental
Avis Rent A Car, 33 N. Capitol Av., 236-1987, **M-21**

Car Repairs
All Star Tire & Auto Service, 534 N. Capitol Av., 269-0500, **M-18**
Cambridge Transmissions Inc., 432 S. Missouri St., 632-3480, **M-33**
Capitol Clutch Corp., 922 N. Capitol Av., 637-2308, **M-14**
Downtown Car Care Center, 540 Virginia Av., 637-2419, **M-30**

Firestone Tire & Service Center, Delaware & Michigan Sts., 634-1346, **M-8**

Fullen Auto & Truck Electric Service, 601 S. West St., 637-8615, **M-33**

Goodyear Auto Service Center, 627 N. Delaware St., 635-1436, **M-8**

Matt's Alignment Service, Inc., 725 N. Capitol Av., 634-3379, **M-14**

Safeway Auto Service, 738 N. Illinois St., 822-4199, **M-14**

Car Sales

Auto Consortium, 646 Virginia Av., 917-1987, **M-30**

Bob's Auto Sales, 704 E. Fletcher Av., 635-6002, **M-23**

Circle Auto Resource, 438 Virginia Av., 638-2886, **M-30**

United Auto Sales, 602 Virginia Av., 263-0366, **M-30**

Car Service Stations

CITGO, SW cnr Ohio & East Sts., **M-11**

Marathon Service Station, SW cnr St. Joseph & Delaware Sts., **M-4**

Multi-Zone, cnr Michigan & Alabama Sts., **M-8**

Speedway, SW cnr Kentucky & West Sts., **M-34**

Car Towing

Delaware & South Towing Service, 310 S. Delaware St., 638-1458, **M-24**

Car Washing

Mike's Express Carwash, 1219 N. Meridian St., 423-2470, **M-13**

Swancy's Auto Laundry, 934 N. Senate Av., 635-0618, **M-15**

Caterers

Crystal Catering, 520 N. New Jersey St., 615-1500, **M-7**

Lockerbie Catering Co., 430 N. College Av., 635-8624, **M-6**

CDs, Cassettes & Records

Luna Music Annex, 433 Massachusetts Av., 917-5862, **M-7**

See also Circle Centre stores listed in Chapter 3

Child Care

Federal Center Day Nursery, 575 N. Pennsylvania St., 226-5487, **M-8**

IUPUI Center for Young Children, 321 N. Limestone St., 274-3508, **M-29**

St. Mary's Child Center, 901 Dr. Martin Luther King Jr. St., 635-1491, **M-15**

Shalom Day Care, 401 N. Delaware St., 635-1994, **M-8**

State Center Day Nursery, 100 N. Senate Av., 233-1776, **M-22**

Wiles Center Day Nursery, 855 N. East St., 637-4316, **M-2**

Chiropractors

Heliport Area Chiropractic, 8 S. New Jersey St., **M-24**

Massachusetts Avenue Chiropractic, 611 Massachusetts Av., 554-0748, **M-6**

Churches

Allen Chapel A.M.E. Church, 627 E. 11th St., 638-9963, **M-2**

Bethel A.M.E. Church, 414 W. Vermont St., 634-7002, **M-19**

Bethesda Missionary Baptist Church, 234 W. Ray St., 638-9470, **M-33**

Cathedral of Praise Bible Way Westside Church, 1030 Central Av., 684-1696, **M-3**

Central Christian Church, 701 N. Delaware St., 635-6397, **M-8**

Christ Church Cathedral, 125 Monument Circle, 636-4577, **M-20**

Christian Science Reading Room, 10 N. Pennsylvania St., 638-0991, **M-20**

Christian Church – Disciples of Christ General Offices, 130 E. Washington St., 635-3100, **M-24**

Church of Jesus Christ of Apostolic Faith, 701 E. McCarty St., 638-1997, **M-30**

Cornerstone Baptist Church, 940 N. Pennsylvania St., **M-13**

First Lutheran Church, 701 N. Pennsylvania St., 635-9505, **M-8**

Greater Gethsemane Missionary Baptist Church, 902 Dr. Martin Luther King Jr. St., 635-4663, **M-16**

Holy Rosary Catholic Church, 520 Stevens St., 636-4478, **M-30**

Lockerbie Square United Methodist Church, 237 N. East St., 637-2716, **M-10**

Metropolitan Baptist Center, 952 N. Pennsylvania St., 687-0075, **M-13**

New Life Christian Fellowship, 720 Dr. Martin Luther King Jr. St., **M-16**

Park Avenue Church of Christ, 620 E. 10th St., 635-5580, **M-2**

Pentecostal Workers Assembly, 708 S. Meridian St., 638-7825, **M-32**

Roberts Park United Methodist Church, 401 N. Delaware St., 635-1636, **M-8**

St. Bridget Catholic Church, 720 Dr. Martin Luther King Jr. St., **M-16**

St. John Catholic Church, 126 W. Georgia St., 637-3941, **M-26**

St. Mary's Catholic Church, 317 N. New Jersey St., 637-3983, **M-11**

St. Philip's Episcopal Church, 720 Dr. Martin Luther King Jr. St., 636-1133, **M-16**

Upper Room Apostolic Church, 1019 Broadway St., 955-1848, **M-2**

Zion Evangelical United Church of Christ, 416 N. East St., 639-5411, **M-7**

Circle Centre Mall

See list of stores in Chapter 3

City Market (222 E. Market St., **M-12**)

Al's City Market Shoe Repair, 639-5518

Abbey's Market, 223-7693

Ameer, 681-8444

Asiana Market, 631-2000

BMV Express

Burda Alterations, 972-8060

Caribbean Spice, 634-9970

CATH, Inc., 374-5744

Cella's Choice, 236-8999

City Market Deli, 258, 8258

City Market Seafood & Meat

Crazy Cajun, The, 236-8999

Dottie's Deli, 635-7473
El Azabache, 822-6280
Enzo Pizza, 266-0498
Fisher of Men Shoe Shine, Inc., 257-2512
Good Stuff, 630-9155
Grecian Garden & Market, 634-0191
Hot Shop, 332-8406
Intellectual Technology, 760-599-8080
Indianapolis Gallery Market, 709-2253
Jewell's Beads & Treasures, 840-4337
Judge's Tip of the Rib Barbeque, 951-2244
Juice Garden, 822-9200
Jumbo's, Inc., 631-5393
Just Cookies, 634-4456
Kasey's Cinnamon Roasted Nuts, 627-7706
Muggins, 910-6191
National Bank of Indianapolis, 261-9000
Perfect Gift, 783-2602
Philadelphia Steak & Fries, 635-1199
Potatoes & More, 972-8060
Prestige Catering, 635-7473
Roly Poly, 951-1433

Clinics & Counseling Centers

Counseling Center, The, 429 E. Vermont St., **M-11**
Gennesaret Free Clinic, 631 E. New York St., 262-5645, **M-10**
Gennesaret Free Clinic Dental & Wellness Ctr., 725 N. Pennsylvania St., 955-0217,
   M-8
Midtown Community Mental Health Center, 964 N. Pennsylvania St., 630-7791,
   M-13
Midtown Mental Health Services (Wishard), 832 N. Meridian St., **M-13**
Occupational Health of Community Health Network, 915 N. Capitol Av.,
   355-2400, **M-14**

Clothing Stores

Dress Barn, 111 Monument Circle (in Bank One Center), 266-9676, **M-20**
Harry Levinson's Warehouse, 427 S. Illinois St., 321-9999, **M-32**
Just Outlet, 38 E. Washington St., 635-6030, **M-20**
Splurge, Inc., 446 Massachusetts Av., 637-3000, **M-7**
See also Circle Centre stores listed in Chapter 3

Clubs

Club Indianapolis, 620 N. Capitol Av., 635-5796, **M-18**
Columbia Club, The, 121 Monument Circle, 767-1361, **M-20**
Gatling Gun Club, 709 N. Illinois St., 631-3535, **M-17**

Indianapolis Athletic Club, 350 N. Meridian St., 634-4331, **M-20**
Indianapolis Press Club, 150 W. Market St., 767-7756, **M-21**
University Club of Indiana, The, 970 N. Delaware St., 638-3571, **M-4**

Coffee Shops

Abbey, The, 771 Massachusetts Av., 269-8426, **M-6**
Bad Ass Coffee Co., The, NE cnr Washington & Meridian Sts., **M-20**
CATH, Inc., City Market, 374-5744, **M-12**
Corner Coffee, 251 E. 11th St., 916-9805, **M-4**
Cornerstone Coffee & Espresso Bar, 1 N. Pennsylvania St., 951-9660, **M-24**
Cups Coffee Shop, 107 N. Pennsylvania St., 951-2223, **M-12A**
Espresso Bar, Nordstrom, 130 S. Meridian St., 636-2121, **M-25**
40 West Coffee Café, 40 W. Jackson Pl., 686-1414, **M-25**
Luxe Café-Mart, 156 E. Market St., 488-8736, **M-12A**
Starbuck's, SW cnr Ohio & Meridian Sts., 635-2000, Ext. 2690, **M-20**
Starbuck's, 55 Monument Circle, 917-1893, **M-20**
Starbuck's, 430 Massachusetts Av., 423-9328, **M-7**
Starbuck's, 645 W. 11th St., 822-3740, **M-16**
Vecino's Coffee Gallery, 542 N. Alabama St., 634-1995, **M-8**
Vic's Downtown Espresso Bar, 627 N. East St., 951-0335, **M-6**

Comedy Clubs

ComedySportz Arena, 721 Massachusetts Av., 951-8499, **M-6**
Crackers Comedy Club, 247 S. Meridian St., 631-3536, **M-25**

Comic Books

Downtown Comics, 11 E. Market St., 237-0397, **M-20**

Computer Dealers

MacExperience, The, 251 S. Meridian St., 916-1630, **M-25**

Computer Service

Circle City Computers, Inc. 901 N. East St., 917-1150, **M-2**
Computer Experts, Inc., 445 N. Pennsylvania St., 833-3000, **M-8**

Condominiums

Avenue, The, 436 Massachusetts Av., 637-8996, **M-7**
Clevelander, The, Ohio St. between New Jersey & Cleveland Sts., 570-4358, **M-11**
Glencoe, The, 627 N. Pennsylvania St., **M-8**
Horace Mann Condominiums, 927 S. Noble St., **M-30**
Hudson, The, New Jersey & Ohio Sts., SW cnr, 499-9999, **M-11** & **M-24A**
Indianapolis Glove Co., 430 N. Park Av., 684-3333, **M-6**
Lockerbie Terrace, 225 N. New Jersey St., 590-7000, **M-11**
Market Square Partners, 251 E. Ohio st., 635-1111, **M-24A**
Meridian Street Lofts, 207 S. Meridian St., **M-25**

Merrill Street Condos, Merrill St. west of Virginia Av., 226-9213, **M-30**
110 E. Washington Condominium Assn., 917-1431, **M-24**
Packard, The, 450 E. Ohio St., 299-9999, **M-11**
Real Silk Lofts, 611 N. Park Av., **M-6**
Six Over Meridian, 141 S. Meridian St., **M-25**
Union Laundry Lofts, 735 Lexington Av., **M-30**

Conference & Convention Centers

Crowne Plaza Hotel and Conference Center at Union Station, 123 W. Louisiana St.,
631-2221, **M-25**
Fletcher Pointe Banquet & Conference Center, 501 Fletcher Av., 635-2266, **M-30**
Indiana Convention Center, 100 S. Capitol Av., 262-3400, **M-26**
University Place Conference Center, 850 W. Michigan St., 274-2700, **M-28**

Consulates

Consulate of Mexico, Union Station, 951-0005, **M-25**

Consultants

Luther Consulting. LLC, 423 Massachusetts Av., 636-0282, **M-7**
Dress For Success Indianapolis, 850 N. Meridian St., 940-3737, **M-13**

Contractors, General

Brandt Construction, Inc., 330 E. St. Joseph St., 638-3300, **M-3**
Jungclaus-Campbell General Contractors, 825 Massachusetts Av., 264-6655, **M-1**
Shiel-Sexton Co., Inc., 902 N. Capitol Av., 423-6000, **M-14**

Contractors, Mechanical

Frank E. Irish, Inc., 625 E. 11th St., 636-0357, **M-2**

Convenience Stores

CITGO, SW cnr Ohio & East Sts., **M-11**
Marathon Service Station, SW cnr St. Joseph & Delaware Sts., **M-4**
Multi-Zone, cnr Michigan & Alabama Sts., **M-8**
Speedway, SW cnr Kentucky & West Sts., **M-34**

Cookies

Just Cookies, City Market, 634-4456, **M-12**
See also Circle Centre stores listed in Chapter 3

Copying & Duplicating Services

A-1 Letter & Print Shop, 417 E. Ohio St., 632-7212, **M-11**
Brand Printing, 155 N. Illinois St., 635-3939, **M-20**
Kinko's, 120 Monument Circle, 631-6862, **M-20**
PIP Printing Center, 445 N. Pennsylvania St., 634-2963, **M-8**
Quick Copy & Design, 151 N. Delaware St., 236-9755, **M-12**
Three-S Reproductions, 643 Massachusetts Av., 637-3773, **M-6**

Couriers

Now Courier, Inc., 111 E. McCarty St., 638-6066, **M-32**

Credit Unions

Indiana Members Credit Union, 136 N. Delaware St., 635-7729, **M-12A**

Dance Clubs

Lotus, 235 S. Meridian St., 951-2174, **M-25**
Tiki Bob's, 231 S. Meridian St., 974-0954, **M-25**

Dancing Instruction

Clara R. Noyes Academy of Ballet Internationale, The, 502 N. Capitol Av.,
635-6080, **M-18**
Red Brick Dance Studio, The, 130? N. Delaware St., 916-4055, **M-12A**

Delicatessens

Asiana Market, City Market, 631-2000, **M-12**
City Market Deli, City Market, 258-8258, **M-12**
Dottie's Deli, City Market, 635-7473, **M-12**
Hoaglin To Go, 448 Massachusetts Av., **M-6**
Shapiro's Delicatessen Cafeteria, 808 S. Meridian St., 631-4041, **M-32**

Dentists

See list in Chapter 7.

Department Stores

Nordstrom, 130 S. Meridian St. (Circle Centre), 636-2121, **M-25**
Old Navy Clothing Store, 110 W. Washington St., 955-8949, **M-21**
Parisian, 1 W. Washington St. (Circle Centre), 971-6310, **M-25**
TJ Maxx, 50 N. Illinois St., 972-0273, **M-21**

Discount Stores

Angelo's Railroad & Truck Salvage, Inc., 201 S. College Av., 634-6552, **M-23**

Drug Rehabilitation Programs

Liberty Hall, 675 E. Washington St., **M-23**

Dry Cleaners

Addie's 45-Minute Cleaners, 960 Indiana Av., 631-6965, **M-16**
Curley's Cleaners, 249 E. 11th St., 634-6523, **M-4**
Deering Cleaners Downtown, 602 N. Capitol Av., 251-6740, **M-18**
Sander's Cleaners, 440 Massachusetts Av., 951-0155, **M-7**
Tuchman Cleaners, 304 E. New York St., 635-5810, **M-11**

Electric Companies & Substations
Citizens Thermal Energy (steam plant), 302 S. West St., **M-34**
IPALCO-Indianapolis Power & Light Co., 1 Monument Circle, 261-8222, **M-20**
IPL Hebrew Substation, 602 W. Ray St., **M-34**
IPL 10th Street Substation, **M-1**

Emergency Services
American Red Cross of Greater Indianapolis, 441 E. 10th St., 684-1441, **M-3**

Engineering Companies
Peeler Engineering, Inc., 724 E. Ohio St., 262-8300, **M-9**
Charlier, Clark & Linard, P.C., 440 N. Meridian St., 624-1600, **M-17**

Event Planning
Savoir Fare, Inc., 719 ¹/₂ Massachusetts Av., 955-8603, **M-6**

Exercise & Physical Fitness Programs
Curves For Women Indy Downtown, 135 N. Pennsylvania St., 685-8206, **M-12A**
IUPUI Natatorium, SE cnr University Blvd. & New York St., **M-27**
National Institute for Fitness & Sport, 250 University Blvd., 274-3432, **M-27**
YMCA at the Athenaeum, 401 E. Michigan St., 685-9705, **M-7**
See also Chapter 8

Farmers' Markets
Indiana Farmers' Co-op Produce, City Market, 222 E. Market St., 634-9266, **M-12**

Federal Offices
Birch Bayh Federal Building & United States Court House, 46 E. Ohio St., **M-20**
Minton Capehart Federal Building, 575 N. Pennsylvania St., **M-8**

FedEx Drop Boxes & Service Counters
Alabama St. inside O'Malia's in Lockerbie Marketplace, 7:30 p.m., M-F, **M-11**
Delaware St. and St. Joseph St.,, NE cnr, 7 p.m. M-F, **M-4**
IUPUI, Union Building, 620 Union Dr., 6:15 p.m. M-F, **M-28**
300 N. Meridian St., **M-20**
Monument Circle Service Counter, to the right of Sprint PCS, 800-463-3339, **M-20**
111 Monument Circle at garage level of Bank One, 8 p.m. M-F, **M-20**
550 W. North St., outside Sigma Theta Tau, 5:30 p.m. M-F, **M-16**
Virginia & Washington Sts., in Jefferson Plaza Bldg., 6 p.m. M-F, **M-24**

Financial Services
Charles Schwab & Co., Inc., 137 N. Meridian St., 800-435-4000, **M-20**
City Securities Corporation, 30 S. Meridian St., 634-4400, **M-25**
Scottrade Financial Services, 2 N. Meridian St., 636-7599, **M-20**

Fire Stations

Indianapolis Fire Department, Station No. 7, Massachusetts Av. at East St., **M-7**

Indianapolis Fire Department, Station No. 13, Ohio St. at West St., **M-22**

Flea Markets

Teapots Flea Market, 922 Massachusetts Av., **M-1**

Florists

Andrews Florists, Inc., 705 E. Market St., 237-3030, **M-23**

Berkshire Florist & Cookies, 7 E. Market St., 423-2841, **M-20**

Enflora, 1 E. Ohio St. (in Bank One Center), 634-3434, **M-20**

Watts Blooming, 615 Massachusetts Av., 736-6839, **M-6**

Indiana Blooms, 938 Indiana Av., 624-0200, **M-16**

Foundations

Athenaeum Foundation, 401 E. Michigan St., 630-4569, **M-7**

Health Foundation of Greater Indianapolis, The, 342 Massachusetts Av.,
630-1805, **M-12**

Historic Landmarks Foundation of Indiana, 1028 N. Delaware St., 639-4534, **M-4**;
& 340 W. Michigan St., **M-19**

Indiana Bar Foundation, 230 E. Ohio St., 269-2415, **M-12**

Framing Shops

A Frame of Mind, 630 Virginia Av., 637-2191, **M-30**

Frame Shop, The, 617 Massachusetts Av., 822-8455, **M-6**

Framed On The Avenue, 808 Ft. Wayne Av., 236-8515, **M-4**

Great Frame Up, The, 612 N. Delaware St., 636-5040, **M-8**

Fraternal Organizations

Scottish Rite Cathedral, Meridian St. between North and Walnut Sts., **M-17**

Masonic Temple Association, 525 N. Illinois St., 635-1657, **M-17**

Funeral Directors

Willis Mortuary, 632 Dr. Martin Luther King Jr. St., 634-5100, **M-16**

Garden Centers

Cit E Scapes Garden Center and Greenhouse, 1230 S. Meridian St., 624-9344,
M-32 (two blocks south of I-70, at Kansas St.)

Urban Gardener, The, 907 E. Michigan St., 267-9005, **M-5 & M-9,** inside Midland
Arts & Antiques Market, E of I-65/70 on Vermont St.

Glass Companies

Harmon Inc – Glass Service, 530 E. Ohio St., 639-6268, **M-10**

Graphic Art Supplies
Repro-Graphics, Inc., 437 N. Illinois St., 637-3377, **M-17**

Graphic Designers
Dean Johnson Design, Inc., 646 Massachusetts Av., 634-8020, **M-6**
Rowland Design, Inc., 701 E. New York St., 636-3980, **M-9**

Greeting Cards
Mary Ann's Hallmark, 15 E. Market St., 635-2544, **M-20**
See also Circle Centre listings, Chapter 3

Grocers
Joe O'Malia Food Market, Lockerbie Marketplace, 320 N. New Jersey St.,
    262-4888, **M-11**
Save-A-Lot, 617 W. 11th St., 635-4970, **M-16**

Halls & Auditoriums
Fletcher Pointe Banquet & Conference Center, 501 Fletcher Av., 635-2266, **M-30**
Mavris Cultural Center, 121 S. East St., 917-9999, **M-23**

Hardware Stores
Fastenal, 130 W. Walnut St., 955-9512, **M-14**
True Value, Lockerbie Marketplace, **M-11**

Health Food
Good Stuff, City Market, 630-9155, **M-12**

Heliport
Indianapolis Downtown Heliport, 51 S. New Jersey St., 955-1751, **M-24**

Hospitals
Indiana University Hospital, 550 University Blvd., 274-5000, **M-28**
Methodist Hospital, 1701 Senate Blvd., 962-2000, **M-13**
Riley Hospital for Children, 702 Barnhill Dr., 274-5000, **M-28**
Wishard Memorial Hospital, 1001 W. 10th St., 639-6671, **M-28**

Hotels & Motels
Adam's Mark Hotel, 120 W. Market St., 972-0600, **M-21**
Best Western City Centre, 418 S. Missouri St., 822-6400, **M-33**
Canterbury Hotel, 123 S. Illinois St., 634-3000, **M-25**
Columbia Club, 121 Monument Circle, 767-1361, **M-20**
Comfort Inn & Suites, 530 S. Capital Av., 631-9000, **M-33**
Courtyard by Marriott, 320 N. Senate Av., 684-7733, **M-19**
Courtyard by Marriott Indianapolis Downtown, 501 W. Washington St.,
    635-4443, **M-27**

Crowne Plaza Hotel and Conference Center at Union Station, 123 W. Louisiana St.,
    631-2221, **M-26**
Day's Inn Downtown, 401 E. Washington St., 637-6464, **M-24**
Embassy Suites Hotel, 110 W. Washington St., 236-1800, **M-21**
Hampton Inn Downtown, 105 S. Meridian St., 261-1200, **M-25**
Hilton Garden Inn Downtown, 10 E. Market St., 955-9700, **M-20**
Hyatt Regency Indianapolis, 1 S. Capitol Av., 632-1234, **M-26**
Indianapolis Athletic Club, 350 N. Meridian St., 634-4331, **M-20**
Indianapolis Marriott Downtown, 350 W. Maryland St., 822-3500, **M-22**
Malibu Suites Hotel, 14 W. Maryland St., 635-4922, **M-25**
Marriott Residence Inn, 350 W. New York St., 822-0840, **M-19**
Omni Severin Hotel Downtown, 40 W. Jackson Pl., 634-6664, **M-25**
Radisson Hotel City Centre, 31 W. Ohio, 635-2000, **M-20**
Renaissance Tower Historic Inn, 230 E. 9th St., 261-1652, **M-4**
Residence Inn by Marriott, 350 W. New York St., 822-0840, **M-19**
University Place Hotel-IUPUI, 850 W. Michigan St., 269-9000, **M-28**
Westin Hotel Indianapolis, The, 50 S. Capitol Av., 262-8100, **M-22**

Household Furnishings

At Home in the City/Silver in the City, 434 Massachusetts Av., 955-9925, **M-7**
Cathedra Furnishings, 878 Massachusetts Av., 423-1446, **M-1**
See also Circle Centre listings in Chapter 3

Ice Cream Stores

Juice Garden, City Market, 822-9200, **M-12**
Rocky Mountain Chocolate Factory, 28 Monument Circle, 687-1322, **M-20**
South Bend Chocolate Company Café, The, 30 Monument Circle, 951-4816, **M-20**

Ice Skating Rinks

Indiana World Skating Academy, 201 S. Capitol Av., 237-5555, **M-26**

Indiana, State of

Bureau of Motor Vehicles License Branch, 531 Virginia Av., 234-0550, **M-30**
Indiana Department of Health, 2 N. Meridian St., 233-1325, **M-20**
Indiana Department of Education, 151 W. Ohio St., 232-6610, **M-21**
Indiana General Assembly, State Capitol: *Senate,* 232-9400. *House of Representatives,*
    232-9600. State Information Center, 233-0800. **M-21**
Indiana Government Center North, 100 N. Senate Av., 232-0800, 234-0225
    (Hispanic), **M-22**
Indiana Government Center South, 302-402 W. Washington St., 232-0800,
    234-0225 (Hispanic), **M-22**
Indiana State Library, 140 N. Senate Av., 232-3675, **M-22**
Public Employees Retirement Fund (PERF), 143 W. Market St., 233-4162, **M-21**
Unemployment Insurance Review Board, 325 W. Washington St., 232-6702, **M-22**

Indiana University

Cancer Research Institute, Barnhill Dr. across from Riley, **M-28**
Education & Research Institute of Indiana University Radiology,
    714 N. Senate Av., **M-15**
Indiana Cancer Pavilion Radiation Oncology, Michigan St. at Barnhill St., **M-28**
Informatics & Communications Technology Complex, SW cnr Michigan &
    West Sts., **M-27**
IUETC: Evan Bayh Center for Economic Development, 351 W. 10th St., **M-15**
IU Hospital & Outpatient Center, 550 University Blvd., 274-5000, **M-28**
IU School of Law, Indianapolis Campus, 530 W. New York St., 274-8523, **M-27**
Regenstrief Health Center, 1050 Wishard Blvd., 630-7400, **M-28**
Van Nuys Medical Science Building, Barnhill Dr. across from Riley, **M-28**

Indianapolis, City of

City-County Building, **M-24**
See also Chapter 10

Insurance Companies

Anthem Blue Cross & Blue Shield, 120 Monument Circle, 488-6000, **M-20**
Anthem Blue Cross & Blue Shield, 220 Virginia Av., 488-6000, **M-24**
Gregory & Appel Insurance, 520 Indiana Av., 634-7491, **M-19**
Safeco Insurance Co., 500 N. Meridian St., 262-6262, **M-17**
State Farm Insurance Service Center, 724 N. Illinois St., 917-7903, **M-14**

Interior Decorators & Designers

Brenner Design, 108 E. Market St., 262-1220, **M-12A**
Forrest McGinniss Interiors, 408 W. Michigan St., **M-19**

Internet Cafes

Abbey, The, 771 Massachusetts Av., 269-8426, **M-6**
Corner Coffee, 251 E. 11th St., 916-9805, **M-4**
Shaker at Schultzies, 363 N. Illinois St., 634-8533, **M-20**
Starbuck's, 430 Massachusetts Av., 423-9328, **M-7**

IUPUI (Indiana University-Purdue University Indianapolis)

Ball Residence Hall, 1226 Medical Dr., **M-28**
Cavanaugh Bookstore, 425 University Blvd., 278-2665, **M-27**
Coleman Hall, 1140 Medical Dr., **M-28**
Fesler Hall, 1120 South Dr., **M-28**
Gatch Clinical Building, 541 Clinical Dr., **M-28**
Graduate Student Townhouses, Limestone St., **M-28**
Herron School of Art, New York St. between Blake & Blackford Sts., **M-27**
Herron School Photo Lab, 222 W. Michigan St., 920-2462, **M-18**
Administration Building, Presidents' Offices, 355 Lansing St., 274-3571, **M-28**
Kelley School of Business, 801 W. Michigan St., 274-2147, **M-27**

Natatorium, 901 W. New York St., 274-3518, **M-27**
Oral Health Research Institute, 415 Lansing St., **M-28**
Physical Plant, Wishard Blvd. at Elmwood St., **M-28**
Post Office, 536 Barnhill Dr., **M-28**
School of Dentistry, 1121 W. Michigan St., 274-7957, **M-28**
School of Education/Social Work, 902 W. New York St., 274-6705, **M-27**
School of Engineering, Science & Technology, 799 W. Michigan St., 274-2533, **M-27**
School of Liberal Arts, 425 University Blvd., 274-3976, **M-27**
School of Physical Education & Tourism Management, 902 W. New York St.,
    274-2248, **M-27**
School of Public & Environmental Affairs, 801 W. Michigan St., 274-4656, **M-27**
Science Building, NW cnr New York & Blackford Sts., **M-27**
Union Building, 620 Union Dr., **M-28**
University College, 815 W. Michigan St., 274-2237, **M-27**
University Library, 755 W. Michigan St., 274-8278, **M-27**

Jazz Clubs
Chatterbox Jazz Club, 435 Massachusetts Av., 636-0584, **M-7**
Slippery Noodle Inn, 372 S. Meridian St., 631-6968, **M-25**

Jewelry Stores
Artisans'-Jewelry for the Joyful Spirit, 880 Massachusetts Av., 423-9579, **M-1**
Goldman Jewelry, 801 S. Meridian St., 684-9435, **M-32**
Indianapolis Gallery Market, City Market, 709-2253, **M-12**
Jewel's Beads & Treasures, City Market, 840-4337, **M-12**
J-Town Good Jewelry, 44 E. Washington St., 632-7651, **M-20**
Windsor Jewelry Co., 16 N. Meridian St., 634-6610, **M-20**

Keys
Al's City Market Shoe Repair & Keys, 2nd Floor, City Market, 639-5518, **M-12**
Welworth Lock Co., 845 N. Illinois St., 634-5067, **M-13**

Labor Organizations
Carpenters Local 60, 531 E. Market St., 632-9780, **M-23**
Indianapolis Musicians Local No. 3, Delaware St. south of Vermont St., **M-12**
Plasterers & Cement Masons Local 692, Fulton & Miami Sts., **M-9**
Teamsters Local Union No. 716, 849 S. Meridian St., 632-9468, **M-32**

Laundromats
Wash N' Glo, 931 S. East St., 423-2294, **M-30**

Leather Supplies
Landwerlen Leather Co., 365 S. Illinois St., 636-8300, **M-25**

Libraries
Indianapolis-Marion County Public Library, Interim Central Location, 202 N. Alabama St., 269-1700, **M-12**
Indianapolis-Marion County Public Library (reconstruction site), St. Clair St. between Meridian & Pennsylvania Sts., **M-13**

Lilly, Eli and Company
Brougher Building, Meridian St. across from Faris Campus, **M-32**
Child Care Center, 20 E. McCarty St., **M-32**
Child Care Center, SW cnr South and East Sts., **M-31**
Corporate Center, Delaware & McCarty Sts., 276-2000, **M-31**
Faris Campus, SW cnr. Meridian & South Sts., **M-32**
Lilly Fitness Center, Meridian St. between Merrill & Norwood Sts., **M-32**

Liquor Stores
Alabama Liquors, 947 N. Alabama St., 634-8792, **M-3**
John's Spirits, Decanters & Fine Wines, 25 N. Pennsylvania St., 637-5759, **M-24**
Lee's Liquors, 811 N. Illinois St., 637-9696, **M-13**

Loans
Countrywide Home Loans, 52 Monument Circle, 423-7752, **M-20**
See also Banks

Locks & Locksmiths
Welworth Lock Co., 845 N. Illinois St., 634-5067, **M-13**

Mail Box Rental & Receiving Services
The UPS Store, 133 W. Market St., 236-0009, **M-21**

Map Stores
Odyssey Map Store, 902 N. Delaware St., 635-3837, **M-4**

Marble & Tile Stores
Chance Brothers Marble & Tile, 114 W. McCarty St., 635-7531, **M-32**

Marion County Facilities
Department of Corrections Work Release Center, 448 W. Norwood St., **M-33**
Marion County Coroner—Dr. Dennis J. Nicholas Institute of Forensic Science, 521 W. McCarty St., 327-4744, **M-34**
Marion County Jail II, 730 E. Washington St., **M-23**
Marion County Processing Center, 752 E. Market St., **M-9**

Martial Arts Instruction
Kelley-Myers Karate & Self Defense, 940 Indiana Av., 266-9276, **M-16**

Mass Transit
Clarian People Mover, connecting Methodist Hospital and IU/Riley/Wishard
    hospitals, **M-15, M-16, M-28**
IndyGo (routes and schedules), 635-3344

Massage Therapy
Massage Therapy, 901 N. East St., 840-8710, **M-2**

Meat Markets
Klemm's German Sausage & Meat Market, 315 E. South St., 632-1963, **M-31**

Medical Laboratories
Clarian Health Downtown Laboratory, 11th St. at the Canal, **M-15**

Memorials & Monuments
Congressional Medal of Honor Memorial, Canal Walk W of West St., 826-1661, **M-27**
Indiana War Memorial Shrine & Museum, Meridian & North Sts., **M-17**
Law Enforcement & Fire Fighters Memorial, 100 N. Senate Av., **M-22**
McCormick's Rock, White River State Park, **M-27**
Soldiers & Sailors Monument, Monument Circle, **M-20**
U.S.S. Indianapolis Memorial, Canal Walk at Walnut St., **M-15**

Mental Health Services
Universal Behavioral Services, 820 Ft. Wayne Av., 684-0442, **M-4**

Movers
Hogan Transfer-Mayflower Agency, 825 E. St. Clair St., 639-9583, **M-1**

Museums
Colonel Eli Lilly Civil War Museum, Monument Circle in the War Memorial,
    232-7615, **M-20**
Eiteljorg Museum Of American Indians & Western Art, 500 W. Washington St.,
    636-9378, **M-27**
Firefighter Museum & Historical Society, 748 Massachusetts Av., **M-6**
Indiana Historical Society, 450 W. Ohio St., 232-1882, **M-22**
Indiana State Museum, 650 W. Washington St., 232-1637, **M-27**
Indianapolis Museum of Contemporary Art, SW cnr Vermont St. & Senate Av., **M-19**
Museum Home of James Whitcomb Riley, 528 Lockerbie St., 631-5885, **M-10**
National Art Museum of Sport at University Place-IUPUI, 850 W. Michigan St.,
    274-3627, **M-28**
NCAA Hall of Champions, 750 W. Washington St., 916-4255, **M-27**

Musical Instrument Sales & Repair
Musicians' Repair & Sales, 332 N. Capitol Av., 635-6274, **M-18**

Neighborhoods
Chatham-Arch, **M-2, M-6**
Fletcher Place, **M-30, M-31**
Lockerbie Square, **M-5, M-6, M-9, M-10**
Market Square, **M-11, M-24A**
Ransom Place, **M-16**
St. Joseph, **M-3, M-4, M-8**

News Dealers
Bookland, 137 W. Market St., 639-9864, **M-21**
Delaware News Co., 130 N. Delaware St., 632-9331, **M-12A**

Newspapers
Indianapolis Star, 307 N. Pennsylvania St., 444-4000, **M-12**

Night Clubs
AJ's Lounge, 551 N. Senate Av., 632-9858, **M-18**
Chatterbox Tavern, 435 Massachusetts Av., 636-0584, **M-7**
Fusion, 603 E. Market St., 638-3004, **M-23**
Kameleon, 120 E. Market St., 964-0400, **M-12A**

Off-Track Betting
Trackside Off-Track Betting, 110 W. Washington St., 656-7223, **M-21**

Office Furniture
Office Furniture Mart of Indianapolis, 220 E. St. Clair St., 636-6696, **M-4**
RJE Business Interiors, 621 E. Ohio St., 293-4051, **M-10**

Office Supplies
Arvey Paper & Office Products, 1021 N. Pennsylvania St., 634-3227, **M-4**

Office/Loft/Studio Space For Rent
Canal Walk Lofts, 836 N. Senate Av., 408-9058, **M-15**
Chatham Center, 901 N. East St., 571-8280, **M-2**
Lockerbie Academy, 429 E. Vermont St., **M-11**
One-Twenty Market Suites, 120 E. Market St., 634-8001, **M-12A**
Stutz Business Center, The, 1060 N. Capitol Av., 488-7373, **M-14**

Optical Goods
Urbane Optical, 429 Massachusetts Av., 396-0003, **M-7**
Shimp Optical Corp., 932 S. Meridian St., 636-4448, **M-32**

Optometrists
Downtown Eye Care, 50 S. Meridian St., Suite 103, 634-9909, **M-25**
Indianapolis Eye Care Center, 501 Indiana Av., 321-1470, **M-19**

Packaging & Shipping Services
The UPS Store, 133 W. Market St., 236-0009, **M-21**

Paint Stores
Porter Paint Co., 952 N. Delaware St., 267-0500, **M-4**
Quality Paint & Glass, 215 N. College Av., 262-8180, **M-9**

Parking Lots & Buildings
AUL Parking Garage, NE cnr Ohio St. & Capitol Av., 636-0215, **M-21**
Bank One Garage, 101 N. New Jersey St., 637-2933, **M-11**
Bank One Garage, East St. between Wabash & Market Sts., Central Parking
    System, 321-3183, **M-11** & **M-24A**
Central Park Garage, 301 N. Illinois St., 237-2961, **M-20**
Circle Centre Parking, 26 W. Georgia St., **M-25**
Circle Centre Parking, 100 S. Illinois St., **M-26**
Circle Centre Parking, 49 W. Maryland St., **M-25**
Claypool Parking Garage, 33 N. Capitol Av., 632-9805, **M-21**
Express Park Garage, 20 N. Pennsylvania St., 231-1385, **M-20**
Express Parking, Inc., 145 E. Market St., 488-7275, **M-24**
Indiana Government Center Parking Facility, entrance from Missouri St. between
    Maryland & Washington Sts., **M-22**
Indiana Government Center Senate Avenue Parking Facility (state employees
    only), **M-22**
130 W. Market St., **M-21**
Pan American Plaza Parking Garage, 201 S. Capitol Av., 237-5790, **M-26**
Penn Park, 35 N. Pennsylvania St., 638-8701, **M-24**
Plaza Park, 109 S. Capitol St., 638-2171, **M-26**
Plaza Parking Garage, 30 W. Vermont St., 916-8533, **M-17**
Side Line Parking, 121 E. Maryland St., 686-0486, **M-24**
Union Station Self Park, 301 S. Meridian St., 266-8842, **M-25**
See also Chapter 9

Parks
Babe Denny Park, Wyoming & Meikel Sts., **M-33**
Capitol Commons, 10 S. Capitol Av., **M-26**
Edna Balz Lacy Family Park, Greer St. between McCarty & Stevens Sts., **M-30**
Military Park, SW cnr West & New York Sts., **M-27**
Ransom Place Park, NW cnr Indiana Av. & Paca St., **M-16**
University Park, NE cnr Meridian & New York Sts., **M-20**
Veterans' Memorial Plaza, Michigan to St. Clair Sts. along Meridian St., **M-17**
White River State Park, W. Washington St. at White River, **M-27**

Pet Services & Supplies

Doggy Daycare, 717 N. Capitol Av., 631-3647, **M-14**
Downtown Veterinarian, 542 E. 11th St., 972-1111, **M-2**
The Rhinestone Collar, 115 E. 9th St., 955-8535, **M-4**
Three Dog Bakery, 444 Massachusetts Av., 238-0000, **M-7**

Pharmacies

CVS Pharmacy, 105 E. Ohio St., 636-5577 (pharmacy), 632-7772 (store), **M-12A**
CVS Pharmacy, 175 N. Illinois St., 636-6664 (pharmacy), 632-1394 (store),
    open to 6:30 p.m. M-Sat, to 5 p.m. Sunday, **M-20**
O'Malia's Pharmacy, 320 N. New Jersey St., 262-2226, **M-11**
Statscript Pharmacy/Chronimed, 342 Massachusetts Av., 631-6000, **M-12**

Photography Studios

Photography Gallery & Studio, 884 Massachusetts Av., 423-9237, **M-1**
Bass Photo Co., Inc., 308 S. New Jersey St., 632-2277, **M-24**

Physicians & Surgeons

See list in Chapter 7.

Pipe Organ Builders

Goulding & Wood Pipe Organs, 823 Massachusetts Av., 637-5222, **M-1**

Pizza Shops

See also Restaurants
Bazbeaux Pizza, 334 Massachusetts Av., 636-7662, **M-12**
Bearno's, 1 N. Pennsylvania St., **M-24**
Circle City Pizza, 627 E. Market St., 632-2862, 532-0285, **M-23**
Domino's Pizza, 907 N. Pennsylvania St., 635-3030, **M-4**
Domino's Pizza, 845 N. Capitol Av., 635-3030, **M-14**
Donato's Pizzeria, Lockefield Commons, 825 W. 10th St., 231-9700, **M-16**
Eh! Formaggio, 30 E. Georgia St., 822-4339, **M-25**
Enzo Pizza, 143 N. Illinois St., 634-1144, **M-20**
Enzo Pizza, City Market, 266-0498, **M-12**
Giorgio's Pizza, 9 E. Market St., 687-9869, **M-20**
Ianni's Greek Pizzeria, 325 S. College Av., 685-0834, **M-23**
Papa John's Pizza, Lockefield Commons, 953 Indiana Av., 632-7272, **M-16**
Pizza Express, Lockefield Commons, 656-6000, **M-16**
Pizza Hut Express, Lockefield Commons, 951 Indiana Av., 632-4238, **M-16**
Pizza Magia, Lockefield Commons, 805 W. 10th St., **M-16** .
Taylor Made Pizza, 940 N. Pennsylvania St., 955-1240, **M-13**

Plumbing Supplies

Economy Plumbing, 625 N. Capitol Av., 264-2240, **M-18**
Service Pipe & Supply, 302 S. New Jersey St., 639-9308, **M-24**

Police Stations

Indianapolis Police Department-Downtown District, 25 W. 9th St., 327-6500, **M-13**
IUPUI Police, Ball Annex, 1232 Michigan St., 274-7971, **M-28**

Printers

Brand Printing & Photo Litho, 155 N. Illinois St., 635-3939, **M-20**
Faulkenberg Printing Co., Inc., 116 W. Michigan St., 638-1359, **M-18**
Kinko's, 120 Monument Circle, 631-6862, **M-20**
Languell Printing Co., 827 S. East St., 632-5647, **M-30**
Litho Press, Inc., 800 N. Capitol Av., 634-6468, **M-14**
Printing Partners, 106 N. Delaware St., 631-5986, **M-12A**
Print Resources, 212 W. 10th St., 833-7000, **M-14**
Repro-Graphics, Inc., 437 N. Illinois St., 637-3377, **M-17**
RPS Printing Services, 425 W. South St., 464-0261, **M-33**

Public Gardens

White River Gardens, W. Washington St. at White River, 630-2001, **M-27**

Public Housing Communities

Indiana Avenue Apartments, 825 Indiana Av., 261-7221, **M-16**
John J. Barton Apartments, 555 Massachusetts Av., 261-7214, **M-7**
John J. Barton Annex Apartments, 501 N. East St., 261-7213, **M-6**
Lugar Tower Apartments, 901 Ft. Wayne Av., 261-7226, **M-3**

Puppet Studios

Peewinkle's Puppet Studio, 25 E. Henry St., 535-4853, **M-32**

Radio Studios

REAL 97.1, 54 Monument Circle, 237-9288, **M-20**
WHHH, 21 E. St. Joseph St., 266-9600, **M-13**
WIBC, 54 Monument Circle, 266-9422, **M-20**
WTLC AM & FM, 21 E. St. Joseph St., **M-13**
WYJZ-FM, 21 E. St. Joseph St., **M-13**

Railroads

Amtrak, 350 S. Illinois St., 263-0550, 800-872-7245, **M-26**

Real Estate Companies

Alig and Associates Inc., 129 W. North St., 639-1533, **M-18**
Avenue Real Estate, 619 Virginia Av., 632-7325, **M-30**
Flock Real Estate Group, 442 Massachusetts Av., 634-6676, 888-500-1085, **M-7**
Mavris Urban Real Estate, 121 S. East St., 917-9999, **M-23**
Real Estate Indy, 614 Massachusetts Av., 972-4717, **M-6**

Recruiting: U.S. Armed Forces
Army-Navy Career Center, 301 N. Illinois St., 803-2859, **M-20**

Recycling Drop-Offs
Lockerbie Marketplace, **M-11**

Religious Goods
Krieg Brothers Religious Supply House, 119 S. Meridian St., 639-3416, **M-25**

Restaurants
See also Pizza Shops
Acapulco Joe's Mexican Foods, 365 N. Illinois St., 637-5160, **M-20**
Aesop's Tables, 600 Massachusetts Av., 631-0055, **M-6**
Agio, 635 Massachusetts Av., 488-0359, **M-6**
Alcatraz Brewing Co., SE cnr Maryland & Illinois Sts., 488-1230, **M-25**
Ameer, City Market, 681-8444, **M-12**
Amici's Downtown Italian Restaurant, 601 E. New York St., 634-0440, **M-10**
Arby's, 45 E. South St., 423-1264 & 423-1716, **M-32**
Au Bon Pain, Lockefield Commons, 901 N. Indiana Av., 624-9123, **M-16**
L.S. Ayres Tea Room at the Indiana State Museum, 650 W. Washington St.,
    232-1637, **M-27**
Bertolini's Authentic Trattoria, SE cnr Maryland & Illinois Sts. (Circle Centre),
    638-1800, **M-25**
Best Taste Chinese Buffet, Lockefield Commons, 917 Indiana Av., 684-1818, **M-16**
Best Yet Restaurant, The, 34 N. Delaware St., 634-7116, **M-24**
Bistro Tchopstix, 251 N. Illinois St., 636-9000, **M-20**
Bosphorus, The, 935 S. East St., 974-1770, **M-30**
Bourbon Street Chicken, 74 W. New York St., 972-9218, **M-20**
Bourbon Street Distillery, 361 Indiana Av., 636-3316, **M-18**
Buca Di Beppo, 35 N. Illinois St., 632-2822, **M-20**
Buffalo Wild Wings, 15 E. Maryland St., 916-9464, **M-25**
Café O Homestyle Oriental, 111 Monument Circle (on Pennsylvania St. side of
    Bank One Center), 756-8000, **M-20**
Canary Café, 621 Ft. Wayne Av., 635-6168, **M-8**
Caribbean Spice, City Market, 634-9970, **M-12**
Cella's Choice, City Market, 236-8999, **M-12**
Champion's Sport Bar, 350 W. Maryland St., 405-6111, **M-22**
Chammp's Restaurant, SE cnr Washington & Illinois Sts. (Circle Centre),
    951-0033, **M-25**
Chancellor's Restaurant/University Place Hotel, 850 W. Michigan St., 231-5221, **M-28**
Chez Jean Bakery Café, Inc., 314 Massachusetts Av., 624-9533, **M-12**
China King, 148 N. Delaware St., 685-8630, **M-12A**
Circle City Bar & Grille, 350 W. Maryland St., 405-6100, **M-22**
City Café, 443 N. Pennsylvania St., 833-2233, **M-8**
City Market Seafood & Meat, City Market, **M-12**

Claddagh Irish Pub, The, 234 S. Meridian St., 822-6274, **M-25**
Coaches, 28 S. Pennsylvania St., **M-25**
Cozy Restaurant & Cocktail Lounge, 20 N. Pennsylvania St., 638-2100, **M-20**
Crazy Cajun, The, City Market, 236-8999, **M-12**
Crossroads Café at the Indiana State Museum, 650 W. Washington St.,
    232-1637, **M-27**
Downtown Olly's Restaurant/Sports Bar, 822 N. Illinois St., 636-5597, **M-14**
Dunaway's Palazzo Ossigeno, 351 S. East St., 638-7663, **M-23**
Eagle's Nest, 1 S. Capitol (atop Hyatt Regency Hotel), 231-7566, **M-26**
El Azabache, City Market, 822-6280, **M-12**
Elbow Room Pub & Deli, 605 N. Pennsylvania St., 635-3354, **M-8**
Elements, 415 N. Alabama St., 634-8888, **M-7**
El Sol de Tala Mexican Restaurante y Cantina, Union Station, 636-8252, **M-25**
English Ivy's, 944 N. Alabama St., 822-5070, **M-4**
Gabriel's Cafeteria & Sandwich Shoppe, 320 N. Meridian St., 635-0132, **M-20**
Grecian Garden & Market, City Market, 634-0191, **M-12**
Greek Islands Restaurant, 906 S. Meridian St., 636-0700, **M-32**
Greek Village, 72 W. New York St., 951-1500, **M-20**
Hardee's, 710 W. 10th St., 634-8441, **M-16**
Hard Rock Café, 49 S. Meridian St., 636-2550, **M-25**
Hard Times Café, 121 W. Maryland St., 916-8800, **M-26**
Hoaglin To Go Café Marketplace, 448 Massachusetts Av., **M-7**
Hooters, 25 W. Georgia St., 267-9637, **M-25**
Hot Tuna Seafood Restaurant, 40 W. Jackson Pl., 687-5190, **M-25**
Houlihan's Restaurant, 111 W. Maryland St., 266-8711, **M-26**
Iaria's Italian Restaurant, 317 S. College Av., 638-7706, **M-23**
Ike & Jonesy's, 17 Jackson Pl., 632-4553, **M-25**
India Garden Restaurant, 143 N. Illinois St., 634-6060, **M-20**
Jaguar Restaurant & Bar, 924 N. Pennsylvania St., 636-2586, **M-13**
Jillian's Entertainment, 141 S. Meridian St., 822-9300, **M-25**
Jimmy Johns Gourmet Sandwiches, 17 N. Pennsylvania St., 635-6112, **M-24**
Judge's Tip of the Rib Barbeque, City Market, 951-2244, **M-12**
Jumbo's, Inc., City Market, 631-5393, **M-12**
Legal Beagle, 20 N. Delaware St., 266-0088, **M-24**
Le Peep Restaurant, 301 N. Illinois St., 237-3447, **M-20**
Living Room Lounge, The, 934 N. Pennsylvania St., 635-0361, **M-13**
Loading Dock Pub, The, 1045 N. Senate Av., 637-2680, **M-14**
Lockerbie Pub, 631 E. Michigan St., 631-9545, **M-6**
Loughmiller's Pub & Eatery, 301 W. Washington St., 638-7380, **M-22**
MacNiven's Scottish-American Restaurant & Bar, 339 Massachusetts Av., **M-12**
Magic Moments Restaurant, 1 N. Pennsylvania St., 822-3400, **M-24**
Malibu on Maryland, 14 W. Maryland St., 635-4334, **M-25**
Metro, 707 Massachusetts Av., 639-6022, **M-6**
Mikado Japanese Restaurant & Sushi Bar, 148 S. Illinois St., 972-4180, **M-26**
Milano Inn, 231 S. College Av., 264-3585, **M-23**

Morton's of Chicago - The Steak House, 41 E. Washington St., 229-4700, **M-25**
Mo's A Place For Steaks, 47 S. Pennsylvania St., 624-0720, **M-24**
Muggins, City Market, 910-6191, **M-12**
Nordstrom Grill, 130 S. Meridian St., 636-2121, **M-25**
Oceanaire Seafood Room, 30 S. Meridian St., 955-2277, **M-25**
Old Point Tavern, The, 401 Massachusetts Av., 634-8943, **M-7**
Old Spaghetti Factory, The, 210 S. Meridian St., 635-6325, **M-25**
Palomino Restaurant Rotisseria Bar, NE cnr Maryland & Illinois Sts., 974-0400, **M-25**
Panda Express, 48 E. Washington St., 637-0338, **M-20**
Payton's Place, 551 Indiana Av., 822-8075, **M-19**
Penn Station East Coast Subs, 24 W. Washington St., 634-7366, **M-20**
P.F. Chang's China Bistro, SE cnr Washington & Illinois Sts. (Circle Centre),
    974-5747, **M-25**
Philadelphia Steak & Fries, City Market, 635-1199, **M-12**
Potatoes & More, City Market, 972-8060, **M-12**
Prestige Catering, City Market, 635-7473, **M-12**
Pullman's Restaurant & Bar, 123 W. Louisiana St., 236-7470, **M-26**
Qdoba Mexican Grill, Lockefield Commons, 907 Indiana Av., 423-3932, **M-16**
Qdoba Mexican Grill, 9 N. Meridian St., 822-0386, **M-20**
Quizno's Classic Subs, 55 Monument Circle, 269-8838, **M-20**
Quizno's Subs, 150 N. Delaware St., 636-0422, **M-12A**
Ralph's Great Divide, 743 E. New York St., 637-2192, **M-9**
Ram Restaurant & Brewery, 140 S. Illinois St., 955-9900, **M-26**
Rathskeller Restaurant, 401 E. Michigan St., 636-0396, **M-7**
R Bistro, 888 Massachusetts Av., 423-0312, **M-1**
Red Eye Café, 250 S. Meridian St., 972-1500, **M-25**
Restaurant at the Canterbury, 123 S. Illinois St., 634-3000, **M-25**
Rock Bottom Restaurant & Brewery, 10 W. Washington St., 681-8180, **M-20**
Roly Poly, City Market, 951-1433, **M-12**
Roly Poly Meridian, 20 N. Meridian St., 634-7515, **M-20**
Ruth's Chris Steak House, 45 S. Illinois St. (Circle Centre), 633-1313, **M-25**
St. Elmo Steak House, 127 S. Illinois St., 635-0636, **M-25**
Saisaki Grill, Lockefield Commons, 913 Indiana Av., 974-1777, **M-16**
Scholars Inn Gourmet Café & Wine Bar, 725 Massachusetts Av., 536-0707, **M-6**
Shula's Steak House, 50 S. Capitol Av., 231-3900, **M-22**
Side Street Deli, 970 Ft. Wayne Av., 624-1500, **M-3**
Slippery Noodle Inn, 372 S. Meridian St., 631-6974, **M-25**
Stars Sandwich Market, 116 N. Delaware St., 822-9999, **M-12A**
Steak 'n Shake, 101 W. Maryland St., 634-8703, **M-26**
Subway, 160 E. Market St., 631-3291, **M-12A**
Subway, 421 N. Alabama St., 636-7881, **M-7**
Subway, Lockefield Commons, 909 Indiana Av., 974-0490, **M-16**
Subway Sandwiches & Salads, 305 W. Washington St., 267-9960, **M-22**
Subway Sandwiches & Salads, 68 W. New York St., 237-2333, **M-20**
Subway Sandwiches & Salads, 28 E. South St., 536-1700, **M-32**

Taco Bell, Lockefield Commons, 951 Indiana Av., 632-4238, **M-16**
Tailgator's, 375 S. Illinois St., 756-7254, **M-25**
Tarkington's, NE cnr Illinois & Georgia Sts., 635-4635, **M-25**
TGI Friday's, 501 W. Washington St., 685-8443, **M-27**
Ugly Monkey, The, 302 S. Meridian St., 636-8459, **M-25**
Vee's Diner, 435 Kentucky Av., 951-2210, **M-34**
Weekdays Express, 36 S. Pennsylvania St., 917-9734, **M-25**
Whistle Stop Inn, The, 375 S. Illinois St., 639-1605, **M-25**
White Castle, 55 W. South St., 423-0014, **M-32**
Wok N Go Chinese, 135 W. Market St., 630-0046, **M-21**
Yats, 659 Massachusetts Av., 686-6380, **M-6**

Retirement Homes
Goodwin Plaza, 601 W. St. Clair St., 636-7218, **M-16**

Schools, Private
Indiana Business College, 550 E. Washington St., 635-7412, **M-23**
Indianapolis Christian School, 620 E. 10th St., 636-4560, **M-2**
21st Century Charter School, 302 S. Meridian St. (Union Station), Suite 201,
    524-3779, **M-25**

Schools, Public
Center for Inquiry (Benjamin Harrison School), 725 N. New Jersey St.,
    226-4202, **M-7**
Indianapolis Public Schools (HQ), 120 E. Walnut St., 226-4000, **M-8**
Indiana University-Purdue University Indianapolis, **M-27, M-28, M-29**
IPS Pacers Academy, Union Station, 226-4080, **M-25**
Key Learning Community K-12 (Thomas Jefferson School), 777 S. White River
    Pkwy. W. Dr., 226-4992, **M-34**

Sculptors & Sculpture Studios
Leah Orr, Sculptor, 926 N. Alabama St., 637-4532, **M-4**
Precious Design Studio, 950 N. Alabama St., 631-6560, **M-4**

Security Services
Securatex, 239 E. Ohio St., 916-2285, **M-12**
Sonitrol of Indianapolis, 219 E. St. Joseph St., 261-2600, **M-4**

Shoe Stores
Stout's Shoes, 318 Massachusetts Av., 632-7818, **M-12**
See also Circle Centre listings in Chapter 3.

Shoe Repair
Al's Shoe Repair, 222 E. Market St., 639-5518, **M-12**
Cento Shoes, 33 S. Meridian St., 632-5710, **M-25**

Shoe Shine
Fisher of Men Shoe Shine, City Market, 257-2512, **M-12**

Sign Makers
Indy Signworks, Inc., 942 S. Meridian St., 631-1500, **M-32**

Social Service Organizations
Blue Triangle Residence Hall, 725 N. Pennsylvania St., 684-0555, **M-8**
Catholic Youth Organization (CYO), 580 Stevens St., 632-9311, **M-30**
Fletcher Place Community Center, 410 S. College Av., 636-3466, **M-30**
Girls Inc. National Resource Center, 441 W. Michigan St., 634-7546, **M-19**
Hispanic Education Center, 580 Stevens St., 632-9311, **M-30**
Hispano-American Service Center, 617 E. North St., 686-6500, **M-6**
Indianapolis Senior Citizens Center, Inc., 708 E. Michigan St., 263-6272, **M-5**
Lighthouse Mission, 520 E. Market St., 636-0209, **M-10**
Lucille Raines Residence, 947 N. Pennsylvania St., 636-3328, **M-4**
Murat Shrine Club., Inc., 502 N. New Jersey St., 686-4194, **M-7**
Ronald McDonald House, 435 Limestone St., 269-2247, **M-28 & M-29**
Salvation Army Adult Rehabilitation Center, 711 E. Washington St., 638-6585, **M-23**
Salvation Army Central City Corps, 234 E. Michigan St., 687-3714, **M-8**
Volunteers of America, 601 N. Capitol Av., 686-5800, **M-18**
Wheeler Mission Ministries, Adm. Ofc., 205 E. New York St., 635-3575, **M-12;**
    Men's Services, 245 N. Delaware St., 687-6795, **M-12**

Sporting Goods
Arena Sporting Goods, Inc., 140 S. College Av., 635-6161, **M-23**

Sports Teams, Professional
Indiana Fever, WNBA, Conseco Fieldhouse, 125 S. Pennsylvania St., 917-2500, **M-24**
Indiana Pacers, NBA, Conseco Fieldhouse, 125 S. Pennsylvania St., 917-2727, **M-24**
Indianapolis Colts, NFL, RCA Dome, 100 S. Capitol Av., 297-7000, **M-26**
Indianapolis Ice, 1202 E. 38th St., 925-4423
Indianapolis Indians, AAA of the Milwaukee Brewers, Victory Field,
    501 W. Maryland St., 269-3545, **M-27**
See also Chapter 5

Stadiums, Arenas & Playing Fields
Conseco Fieldhouse, 125 S. Pennsylvania St., 917-2500, **M-24**
IUPUI Track & Soccer Stadium, New York St. west of University Blvd., **M-28**
RCA Championships Tournament Office, 815 W. New York St., 632-1111, **M-27**
RCA Dome, 100 S. Capitol Av., 262-3400, **M-26**
Victory Field, 501 W. Maryland St., 269-3542, **M-27**

Stamps for Collectors
The Stamp Shop, 614 Massachusetts Av., 631-0631, **M-6**

Storage Services
Storage USA, 501 N. Fulton St., 635-2126, **M-5**
Shurgard Storage Center, 933 N. Illinois St., 974-0905, **M-13**

Symphony Orchestras
Indianapolis Symphony Orchestra, 45 Monument Circle: Box Office, 639-4300;
    ISO Administrative Offices, 32 E. Washington St., 262-1100, **M-20**

Tailors
Burda Alterations, City Market, 3rd Floor, 972-8060, **M-12**
Leon Tailoring Co., Inc., 809 N. Delaware St., 634-8559, **M-4**
Mina Tailoring Tuxedo & Fine Men's Apparel, 333 E. Ohio St., 631-2702, **M-11**

Tanning Salons
The Gazebo, Inc., 427 Massachusetts Av., 262-9666, **M-7**
Sun Gods, 139 E. Ohio St., 685-2848, **M-12A**
Wash N' Glo, 931 S. East St., 423-2294, **M-30**

Taverns
Alcatraz Brewing Co., SE cnr Maryland & Illinois Sts., 488-1230, **M-25**
Basey's Road Hog Saloon, 419 S. West St., 637-4514, **M-33**
Bourbon Street Distillery, 361 Indiana Av., 636-3316, **M-18**
Capitol Bar, 120 W. Market St., 972-0600, **M-21**
Champion's Sport Bar, 350 W. Maryland St., 405-6111, **M-22**
Charlie & Barney's Saloon, 225 E. Ohio St., 637-5851, **M-12**
Circle Bar Saloon, 148 E. Market St., 917-0042, **M-12A**
Claddagh Irish Pub, 234 S. Meridian St., 822-6274, **M-25**
Coaches, 28 S. Pennsylvania St., **M-25**
Downtown Olly's Restaurant/Sports Bar, 822 N. Illinois St., 636-5597, **M-14**
Dugout Bar, 621 Virginia Av., **M-30**
Elbow Room Pub & Deli, 605 N. Pennsylvania St., 635-3354, **M-8**
501 Tavern, 501 N. College Av., 632-2100, **M-5**
Front Page Sports Bar & Grill, 310 Massachusetts Av., 631-6682, **M-12**
Howl at the Moon Piano Bar, 141 S. Meridian St., **M-25**
Ike & Jonesy's, 17 Jackson Pl., 632-4553, **M-25**
Living Room Lounge, The, 934 N. Pennsylvania St., 635-0361, **M-13**
Loading Dock Pub, The, 1045 N. Senate Av., 637-2680, **M-14**
Lockerbie Pub, 631 E. Michigan St., 631-9545, **M-6**
Metro, 707 Massachusetts Av., 639-6022, **M-6**
Mike's Bar, 802 S. West St., 635-0921, **M-34**
Nick Iaria Tavern, 317 S. College Av., 638-7706, **M-23**
Nicky Blaine's Martinis and Fine Cigars, 7 N. Meridian St., 638-5588, **M-20**

Old Point Tavern, Inc., 401 Massachusetts Av., 634-8943, **M-7**
Olives, Omni Severin Hotel, 40 Jackson Pl., **M-25**
Pub 745, 745 Massachusetts Av., **M-6**
Pub Indianapolis, The, 30 E. Georgia St., 822-9730, **M-25**
Ram Restaurant & Brewery, 140 S. Illinois St., 955-9900, **M-26**
Red Garter Gentleman's Club & Cigar Lounge, 437 S. Illinois St., 637-0829, **M-32**
Slippery Noodle Inn, 372 S. Meridian St., 631-6974, **M-25**
Tailgator's, 375 S. Illinois St., 756-7254, **M-25**
Ugly Monkey, The, 302 S. Meridian St., 636-8459, **M-25**
Whistle Stop Inn, The, 375 S. Illinois St., 639-1605, **M-25**

Tax Preparers
H&R Block, 16 N. Pennsylvania St., 636-4885, **M-20**

Taxis & Limos
AAA Best, 377-0000
Carey Limo, 241-7100
Checker, 574-4444
Indy Airport Taxi, 381-1111
Indy Flyer, 574-4444
Indy Star, 244-9999
Mercury, 636-0000
WWCS, 809-1055
Yellow Cab, 487-7777

City taxi fares in 2004: $5 within Downtown Zone; otherwise, $1.25 first one-fifth mile; 40 cents every one-fifth mile thereafter; 40 cents per minute waiting time.

Telephone Services
Nextel Sales & Service, Delaware St. N of St. Clair St., **M-4**
SBC, 220 N. Meridian St., 800-257-0902, **M-20**
Sprint PCS, 120 Monument Circle, 655-1000, **M-20**
Talking Heads Communications, 615 Virginia Av., 634-3446, **M-30**

Television Studios
WDNI-TV, Channel 65, 21 E. St. Joseph St., 266-9600, **M-13**
WTHR, Channel 13, 1000 N. Meridian St., 636-1313, **M-13**

Tennis Centers
Indianapolis Tennis Center at IUPUI, 150 University Blvd., 278-2100, **M-27**

Theatres-Cinema
IMAX Theater, 650 W. Washington St. (at Indiana State Museum), 233-4629, **M-27**
United Artists Theatres, SE cnr Illinois & Maryland Sts. (at Circle Centre),
    237-6356, **M-25**

Theatres-Stage
American Cabaret Theatre, 401 E. Michigan St., 631-0334, **M-7**
ComedySportz of Indianapolis, 721 Massachusetts Av., 951-8499, **M-6**
Indianapolis Repertory Theater (IRT), 140 W. Washington St., 635-5252, **M-21**
Madame Walker Theater Center, Inc., 617 Indiana Av., 236-2099, **M-16**
The Murat Centre, 502 N. New Jersey St., 231-0000, **M-7**
Phoenix Theatre, 749 N. Park Av., 635-7529, **M-6**
Theatre on the Square, 627 Massachusetts Av., 637-8085, **M-6**
See also Chapter 6.

Thrift Stores
Salvation Army Thrift Store, 725 E. Washington St., 236-1255, **M-23**

Ticket Services
TicketCentral, Indianapolis Artsgarden, Washington & Illinois Sts., 624-2563,
    M-25 & M-26
Wholesale Ticket Service, 36 S. Pennsylvania St., 916-0100, **M-25**

Title Companies
Lawyers Title Insurance Corp., 140 E. Washington St., 633-2933, **M-24**
Title First Agency, Inc., 151 N. Delaware St., 916-8650, **M-12**

Tobacco Stores
Hardwicke Pipe & Tobacco, 24 N. Meridian, 635-7884, **M-20**

Travel Agents
Ross & Babcock Travel, 54 Monument Circle, 635-8512, **M-20**

Typewriter Repair
King Typewriter Agency, Inc., 828 Ft. Wayne Av., 632-4066, **M-4**

Uniforms
U.S. Uniform & Supply, 815 N. Delaware St., **M-4**

United Parcel Service (UPS) Drop Box Locations
Alabama St. inside O'Malia's at Lockerbie Marketplace, 8 p.m. M-F, **M-12**
11th St. between Broadway & College, 6 p.m. M-F, **M-2**
350 S. Illinois St., at Greyhound Package Express, 267-3054, **M-26**
Indiana Av. at Madame C. J. Walker Building, 7:45 p.m. M-F, **M-16**
IUPUI, Union Building, 620 Union Dr., 7 p.m. M-F, **M-28**
111 Monument Circle, garage level of Bank One, 8 p.m. M-F, **M-20**
Union Station, 302 S. Meridian St., 7 p.m. M-F, **M-25**
Virginia & Washington Sts., in Jefferson Plaza Bldg., 5:30 p.m. M-F, **M-24**

U. S. Armed Forces

Army/Navy Career Center, New York St. just east of Illinois St., **M-20**
Indiana National Guard Recruiting Office, SW cnr Walnut St. & Ft. Wayne Av., **M-8**
Tyndall Armory, 711 N. Pennsylvania St., **M-8**

U. S. Postal Service

Circle City Station, 456 N. Meridian St., Indianapolis, IN 46204, 800-275-8777, **M-17**
Andrew Jacobs Jr. Post Office (Main P.O.), 125 W. South St., Indianapolis, IN 46206,
    800-275-8777, **M-32**

U. S. Postal Service (USPS) Drop Box Locations

Alabama & Michigan Sts., NW cnr., 3:15 p.m. M-F, 11:45 a.m. Sat, **M-8**
Bates St. outside 748 E. Bates St., 1 p.m. & 5:30 p.m. M-F, 1 p.m. Sat, **M-23**
Broadway & 10th St., SW cnr., 3:15 p.m. M-F, **M-2**
Capitol Av. on W side of Main P.O. 7, 9 a.m., 12 noon, 1:30, 3, 4, 5, 6, 7 p.m. M-F;
    9 a.m., 1:30, 4, 6 p.m. Sat. **M-32**
Capitol Av. & 10th St., NW cnr., 1:15 p.m. M-F, 11:15 a.m. Sat, **M-14**
Capitol Av. & 9th St., NW cnr., 1:15 & 5:40 p.m. M-F, 11:15 a.m. Sat, **M-14**
Capitol Av. & St. Clair St., SW cnr., 5:40 p.m. M-F, 11:15 a.m. Sat, **M-14**
Delaware St. N of St. Joseph St., 5:45 p.m. M-F, **M-4**
Delaware & Vermont Sts., SE cnr., 4:30 p.m. M-F, 11:15 a.m. Sat, **M-12**
11th Street outside Indy's College Bookstore, 1 p.m. M-F, 1 p.m. Sat, **M-16**
Illinois St. on E side of Main P.O. 7, 9 a.m., 12 noon, 1:30, 3, 4, 5, 6, 7 p.m. M-F;
    9 a.m., 1:30, 4, 6 p.m. Sat. **M-32**
Illinois & Market Sts., SE cnr., 5:30 p.m. M-F, 1 p.m. Sat, **M-20**
Illinois & 10th Sts., SE cnr., 12 & 5 p.m. M-F, 11:15 a.m. Sat, **M-13**
Indiana Av. & Blake St., SW cnr., 1 p.m. M-Sat, **M-16**
Indiana Av. at Madame C. J. Walker Building, 1 p.m. M-F, 1 p.m. Sat, **M-16**
IUPUI, Union Building, 620 Union Dr., 11:15 a.m. & 3:45 p.m. M-F, **M-28**
Meridian & Georgia Sts., NE cnr, 11:30 a.m. & 5:30 p.m. M-F, 12 Noon Sat, **M-25**
Meridian & Louisiana Sts., NW cnr., 5:30 p.m. M-F, 12:15 p.m. Sat, **M-25**
Meridian & Michigan Sts., SW cnr. Collection inside Circle City Station, 6 p.m. M-F,
    2:30 p.m. Sat, **M-17**
Monument Circle outside Anthem, 5 p.m. M-F, 11 a.m. Sat, **M-20**
Pennsylvania St., E side, between New York and Ohio Sts., 3, 5, & 6:45 p.m. M-F,
    11:45 a.m. & 5:30 p.m. Sat, **M-12**
Pennsylvania & Virginia Sts., SE cnr, 5 p.m. M-F, 11 a.m. Sat, **M-24**
Pennsylvania St. W side, between Maryland & Chesapeake Sts., 11:45 a.m. &
    5 p.m. M-F, 11 a.m. Sat, **M-25**
Vermont & Pennsylvania Sts., NE cnr., 5 p.m. M-F, 4:15 p.m. Sat, **M-8**
Virginia Av. outside Calvin Fletcher Apartments, 3 & 5:15 p.m. M-F, 2 p.m. Sat, **M-30**
Virginia & Washington Sts., in Jefferson Plaza Bldg., 5:15 p.m. M-F, **M-24**
Washington St. outside 32 E. Washington, 1 & 4 p.m. M-F, 12 p.m. Sat, **M-20**
Washington & New Jersey Sts., SE cnr, 1 p.m. M-F, 12 Noon Sat, **M-24**

Upholstery Fabric

Mayer-Paetz, Inc., 321 S. Alabama St., 267-2626, **M-24**

Variety Stores

Family Dollar, 611 W. 11th St., 634-7869, **M-16**
H&H Mart, 10 E. Washington St., 637-4321, **M-20**

Veterinarians

Downtown Veterinarian, 542 E. 11th St., 972-1111, **M-2**

Video Stores

Classic Video, 745 N. Illinois St., 632-4211, **M-17**
Hollywood Video, 645 W. 11th St., 453-0562, **M-16 0 1**
Mass Ave Video, 425 Massachusetts Av., 951-7195, **M-7**

Wineries

Easley Winery, 205 N. College Av., 636-4516, **M-9**

Zoos

Indianapolis Zoo, W. Washington St. at White River, 630-2001, **M-27**

Maps

Finding Your Way Around Downtown Indy

The maps in this chapter work with the Directory, Chapter 11, to help you find what you're looking for downtown. Each of the alphabetical references in the Directory ends with an **M** number, indicating the map page where you can find the restaurant, store, office, museum, park, etc., that you're seeking.

Use the large-scale map on the last page of this book to zero-in on particular neighborhoods downtown.

Map Key:

⑮   A circled number is a street address. In general, addresses are given at the corners of blocks to show the range of street numbers on the block. On longer blocks, mid-block addresses may also be given.

⊠   This is a mailbox or an express delivery drop box.

$ This is an ATM machine.

➜   Arrows indicate the direction of street traffic.

M1

I-70 & I-65

I-70 & I-65

TO CARMEL

MONON TRAIL

CHATHAM MANOR
708

11TH ST

EDISON SUBSTATION (IPL)

10TH ST

(OLD) COCA-COLA BOTTLING CO.

BELLEFONTAINE AV

I.P.S. SERVICE CENTER

R BISTRO

SCHOOL BUS PARKING LOT

PHOTOGRAPHY GALLERY
THREE DOT GLASS
ARTISANS
CATHEDRA
MC FEE GALLERY
KUABA
BOCA LOCA

858

THE BIKE SHOP
922
TEA POTS FLEA MARKET

883

CENTER TWP TRUSTEE
LEGENDS SALON
JUNGCLAUS-CAMPBELL GEN'L CONT.

COLLEGE AV

MASSACHUSETTS AV

870

823

GOULDING&WOOD PIPE ORGAN BUILDERS

HOGAN MAYFLOWER

DAVIDSON ST

ST CLAIR ST

© 2004 C.A.

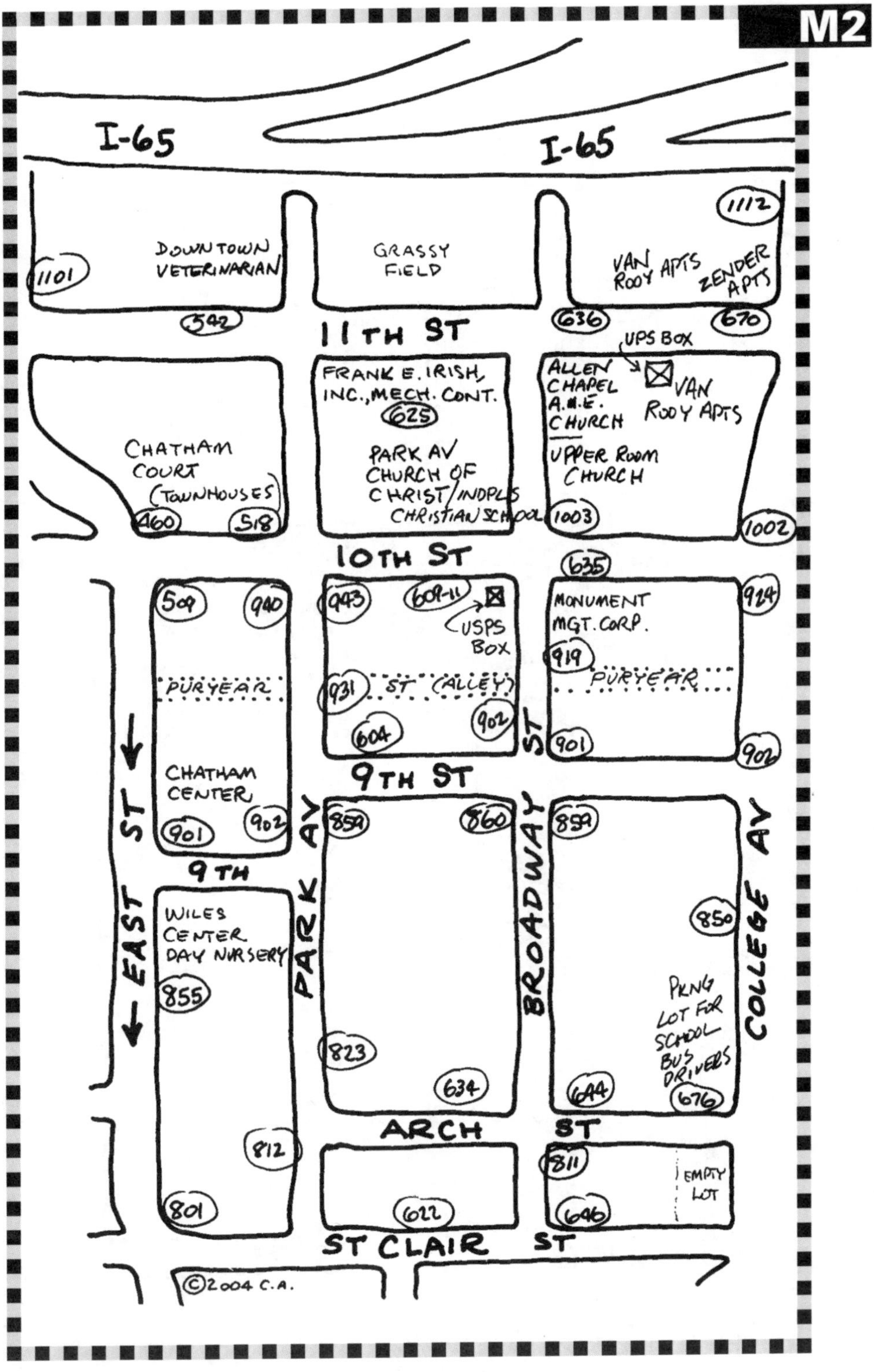

I-65
I-65
1112
1101
DOWNTOWN VETERINARIAN
GRASSY FIELD
VAN ROOY APTS
ZENDER APTS
542
636
670
11TH ST
UPS BOX
FRANK E. IRISH, INC., MECH. CONT.
625
PARK AV CHURCH OF CHRIST/INDPLS CHRISTIAN SCHOOL
ALLEN CHAPEL A.M.E. CHURCH
VAN ROOY APTS
UPPER ROOM CHURCH
CHATHAM COURT (TOWNHOUSES)
460
518
1003
1002
10TH ST
635
509
940
943
609-11
USPS BOX
MONUMENT MGT. CORP.
924
919
PURYEAR
931
ST (ALLEY)
PURYEAR
902
604
901
902
9TH ST
CHATHAM CENTER
902
901
859
860
859
9TH
WILES CENTER DAY NURSERY
855
850
PKNG LOT FOR SCHOOL BUS DRIVERS
823
634
644
676
EAST ST
PARK AV
BROADWAY ST
COLLEGE AV
ARCH ST
812
811
EMPTY LOT
801
622
646
ST CLAIR ST
©2004 C.A.

M3

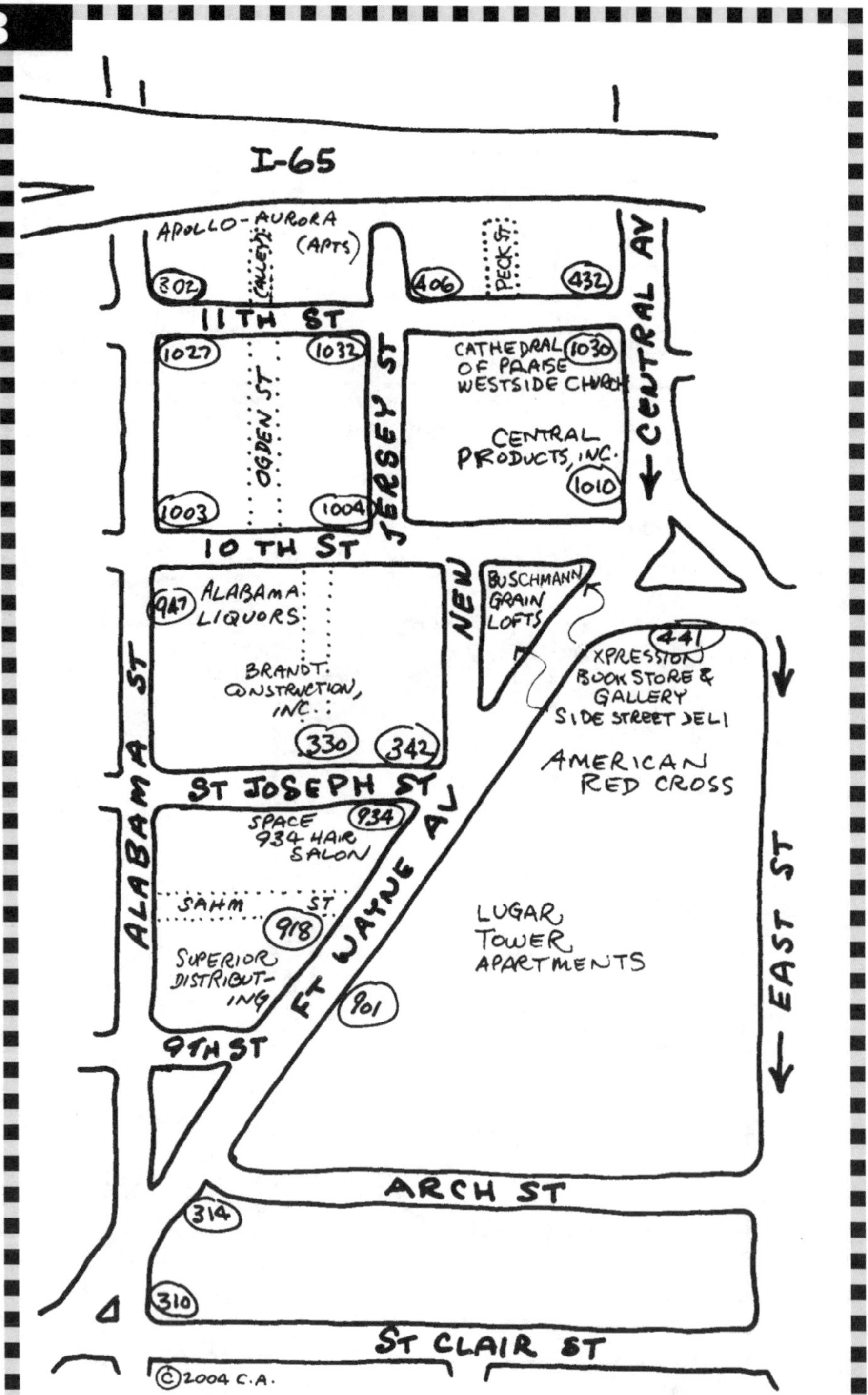
I-65
APOLLO-AURORA
(APTS)
(ALLEY)
PECK ST.
302
406
432
11TH ST
CENTRAL AV
1027
1032
1030
CATHEDRAL OF PRAISE WESTSIDE CHURCH
OGDEN ST
JERSEY ST
CENTRAL PRODUCTS, INC.
1010
1003
1004
10 TH ST
NEW
BUSCHMANN GRAIN LOFTS
947
ALABAMA LIQUORS
BRANDT CONSTRUCTION, INC.
441
XPRESSION BOOK STORE & GALLERY
SIDE STREET DELI
330
342
AMERICAN RED CROSS
ST JOSEPH ST
934
SPACE 934 HAIR SALON
ALABAMA ST
FT WAYNE AV
SAHM ST
918
LUGAR TOWER APARTMENTS
EAST ST
SUPERIOR DISTRIBUTING
901
9TH ST
ARCH ST
314
310
ST CLAIR ST
©2004 C.A.

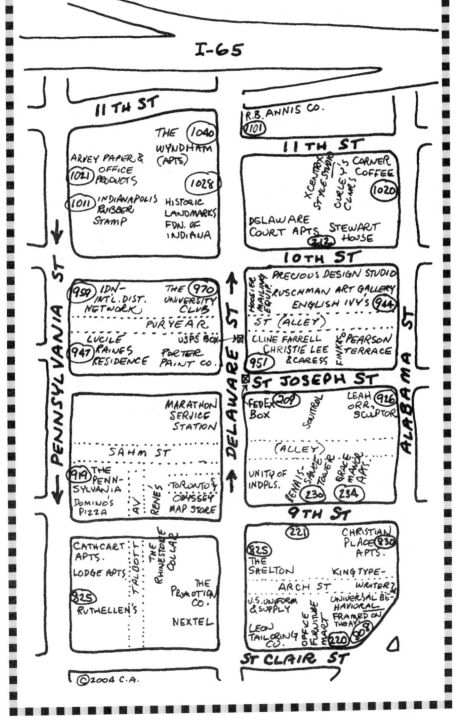

I-65

11TH ST

R.B. ANNIS CO.
101

11TH ST

THE WYNDHAM (APTS.) 1040

ARVEY PAPER & OFFICE PRODUCTS 1021

1028

1011 INDIANAPOLIS RUBBER STAMP

HISTORIC LANDMARKS FDN. OF INDIANA

X CENTRIX STYLE STUDIO
CURLEY'S CORNER COFFEE CLINICS 1020

DELAWARE COURT APTS STEWART HOUSE 212

10TH ST

959 IDN- INTL. DIST. NETWORK

THE UNIVERSITY CLUB 970

PURYEAR

947 LUCILE RAINES RESIDENCE

USPS BOX

PORTER PAINT CO.

HOOSIER MAILING EQUIP.

PRECIOUS DESIGN STUDIO

RUSCHMAN ART GALLERY

ENGLISH IVY'S 944

ST (ALLEY)

951 CLINE FARRELL CHRISTIE LEE & CARESS

FINKRO

PEARSON TERRACE

PENNSYLVANIA ST

DELAWARE ST

St JOSEPH ST

MARATHON SERVICE STATION

FEDEX 209 BOX

SQUIRREL

LEAH ORR, SCULPTOR 926

SAHM ST

(ALLEY)

919 THE PENN-SYLVANIA

RENES AV

TORONTO & ODYSSEY MAP STORE

UNITY OF INDPLS.

RENAISSANCE TOWER 230

GRACE MANOR APTS. 234

DOMINO'S PIZZA

ALABAMA ST

9TH ST

221

CHRISTIAN PLACE APTS. 830

CATHCART APTS.

825 THE SHELTON

KING TYPE-WRITER?

LODGE APTS.

TALBOTT

THE RHINESTONE COLLAR

ARCH ST

825 RUTHELLEN'S

THE PROMOTION CO.

NEXTEL

U.S. UNIFORM & SUPPLY

LEON TAILORING CO.

OFFICE FURNITURE MART

UNIVERSAL BE-HAVIORAL FRAMED ON THE BAY

220 808

St CLAIR ST

© 2004 C.A.

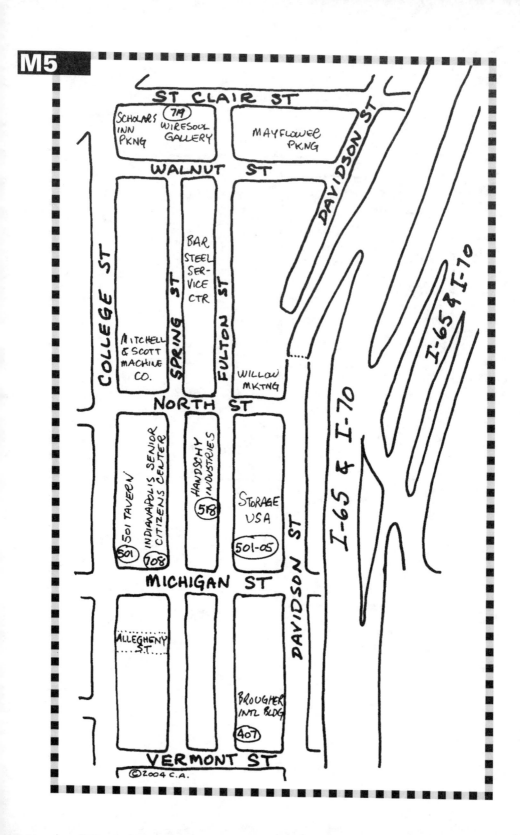

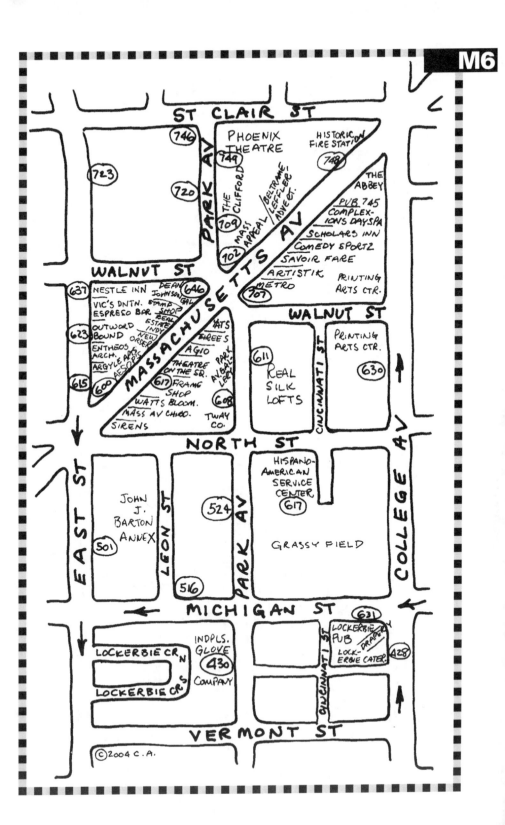

ST CLAIR ST

PARK AV

746

723

720

PHOENIX THEATRE

HISTORIC FIRE STATION

749

748

THE CLIFFORD

709

102

MASS APPEAL

BELTRAME/LEFFLER/ADVE ET.

MASSACHUSETTS AV

THE ABBEY

PUB 745

COMPLEX-IONS DAYSPA

SCHOLARS INN

COMEDY SPORTZ

SAVOIR FARE

ARTISTIK

METRO

707

PRINTING ARTS CTR.

WALNUT ST

NESTLE INN

637

VIC'S DNTN. ESPRESO BAR

OUTWORD BOUND

623

ENTHEOS ARCH.

ARGYLE ARTS

AESOPS

615

600

DEAN JOHNSON GAL.

STAMP SHOP

REAL ESTATE INDY.

NEW ORDER

AGIO

THEATRE ON THE SR.

617

FRAME SHOP

WATTS BLOOM.

MASS AV CHIRO.

SIRENS

6A6

YATS

THREES

PARK AV BAL. LERY

608

TWAY CO.

WALNUT ST

CINCINNATI ST

PRINTING ARTS CTR.

630

611

REAL SILK LOFTS

NORTH ST

EAST ST

LEON ST

JOHN J. BARTON ANNEX

501

524

516

PARK AV

HISPANO-AMERICAN SERVICE CENTER

617

GRASSY FIELD

COLLEGE AV

MICHIGAN ST

631

LOCKERBIE CR N

LOCKERBIE CR S

INDPLS. GLOVE

430

COMPANY

CINCINNATI ST

LOCKERBIE PUB

DRAPERY

LOCK-ERBIE CATER.

A28

VERMONT ST

© 2004 C. A.

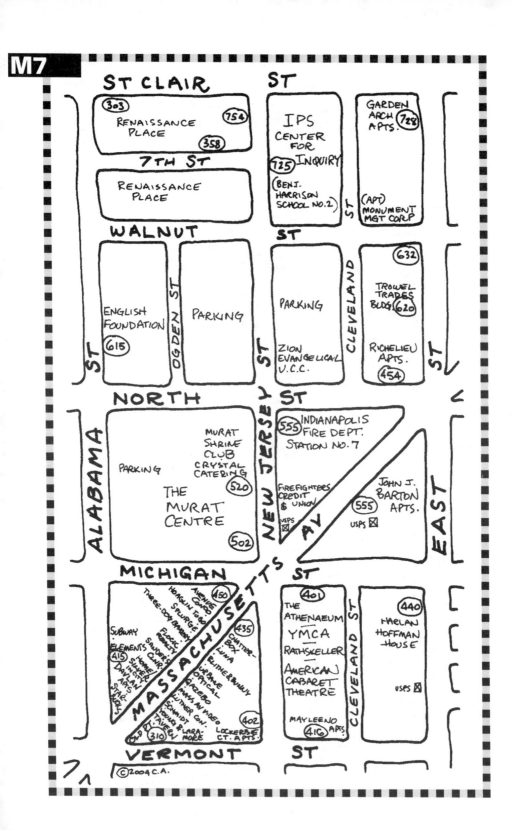

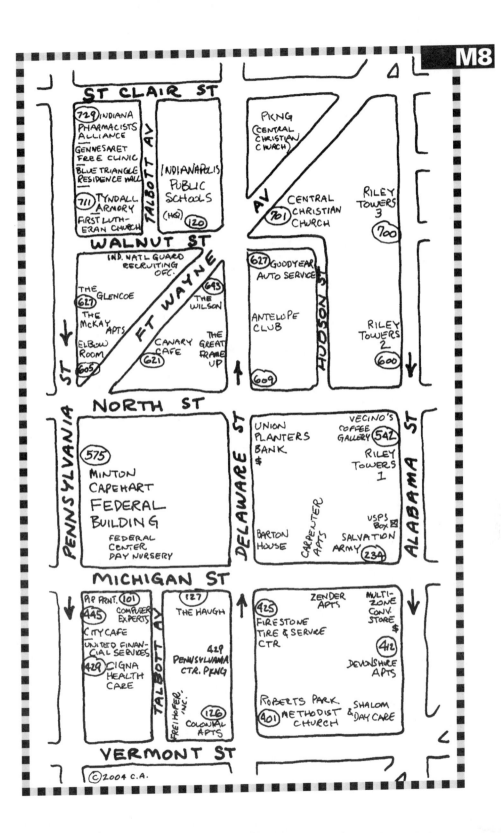

M8

© 2004 C.A.

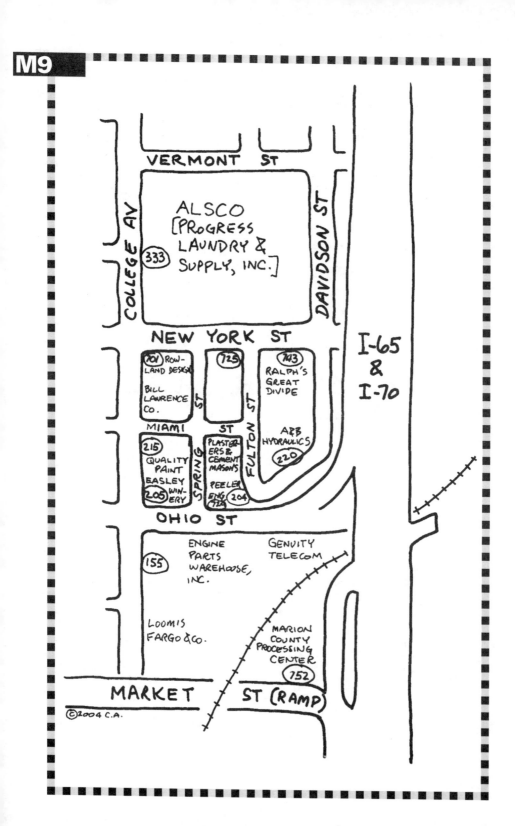

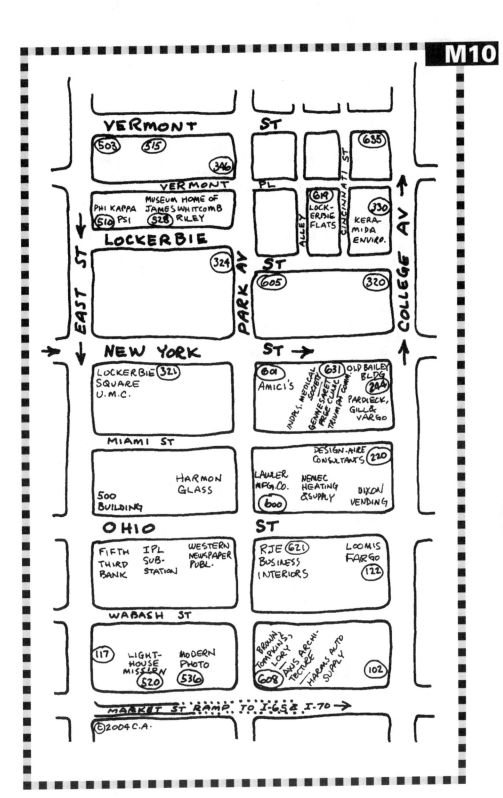

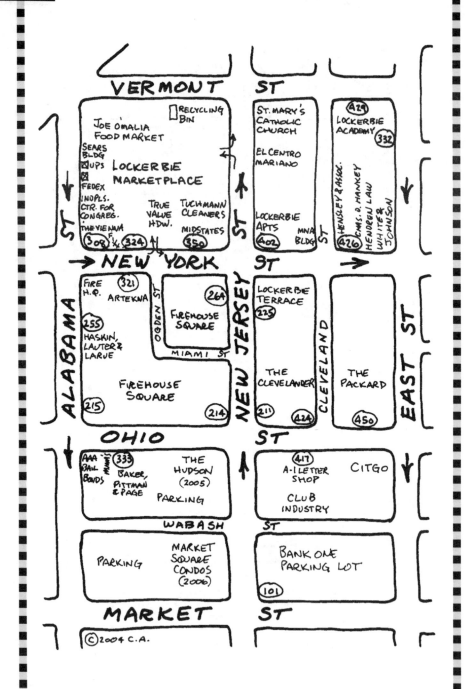

VERMONT ST

RECYCLING BIN

JOE O'MALIA FOOD MARKET

SEARS BLDG
UPS
FEDEX

LOCKERBIE MARKETPLACE

INDPLS. CTR. FOR CONGRES.
THE VIENNA

TRUE VALUE HDW.

TUCHMANN CLEANERS

MIDSTATES

308 324 350

ST. MARY'S CATHOLIC CHURCH

EL CENTRO MARIANO

LOCKERBIE APTS

402

MNA BLDG

429 LOCKERBIE ACADEMY 332

HENSLEY & ASSOC.
CHAS. D. HANKEY
HENDREN LAW
WHITE & JOHNSON

426

NEW YORK ST

ALABAMA ST

FIRE H.Q. 321 ARTEKNA

255 HASKIN, LAUTER & LARUE

OGDEN ST

264 FIREHOUSE SQUARE

MIAMI ST

FIREHOUSE SQUARE

215   214

LOCKERBIE TERRACE
225

THE CLEVELANDER

211   424

NEW JERSEY ST

CLEVELAND ST

THE PACKARD

450

EAST ST

OHIO ST

AAA BAIL BONDS
MIAMI
333 BAKER, PITTMAN & PAGE

THE HUDSON (2005)

PARKING

417 A-1 LETTER SHOP

CLUB INDUSTRY

CITGO

WABASH ST

PARKING

MARKET SQUARE CONDOS (2006)

BANK ONE PARKING LOT

101

MARKET ST

© 2004 C.A.

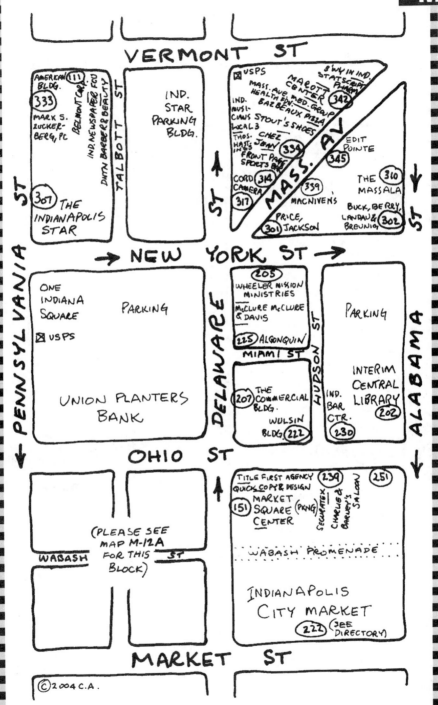

VERMONT ST

AMERICAN BLDG. 111 333
MARK S. ZUCKER-BERG, PC
307 THE INDIANAPOLIS STAR

BELMONT CORP.
IND. NEWSPAPER FCU
DWTN BARBER & BEAUTY

TALBOTT ST

IND. STAR PARKING BLDG.

ST

PENNSYLVANIA ST

☒ USPS
MASS. AVE. MED. GROUP
HEALTH EDN.
IND. MUSI-CIANS LOCAL 3
THOS. HAS INES
FRONT PAGE SPORTS BAR
CORD CAMERA 314 317
MACOTT CENTER
S WY IN IND. STATSCRIP PHARM
342
BAZBEAUX PIZZA
STOUT'S SHOES
CHEZ J-DAN 334
339 MACNIVEN'S
PRICE, 301 JACKSON

MASS. AV

EDIT POINTE 345
THE 310 MASSALA
BUCK, BERRY, LANDAU & BREUNIG 302

ALABAMA ST

→ NEW YORK ST →

ONE INDIANA SQUARE
☒ USPS
UNION PLANTERS BANK

PARKING

205
WHEELER MISSION MINISTRIES
McCLURE McCLURE & DAVIS
225 ALGONQUIN
MIAMI ST
207 THE COMMERCIAL BLDG.
WULSIN BLDG. 222

DELAWARE ST

HUDSON ST

IND. BAR CTR. 230

PARKING

INTERIM CENTRAL LIBRARY 202

OHIO ST

WABASH
(PLEASE SEE MAP M-12A FOR THIS BLOCK)
ST

↑

TITLE FIRST AGENCY 239 251
QUICK COPY & DESIGN
MARKET 151 SQUARE (PKNG) CENTER

SECURATEX
CHARLIE & BARNEY'S SALOON

WABASH PROMENADE

INDIANAPOLIS CITY MARKET
222 (SEE DIRECTORY)

MARKET ST

© 2004 C.A.

M12A

OHIO ST

135 N.
PENNSYLVANIA
⑬⑤ BUILDING

CVS
PHARMACY

SAHM'S AT THE PLAZA

FIRST INDIANA
BANK $

CURVES

CUPS COFFEE SHOP

FORBES, SCHMITT & KOTZAN

SUN GODS

INTER DESIGN

⑬① QUZNO'S
SUBS

CHINA KING

SCHNORR, MAIER
& OLVEY

⑭⑧

$
INDIANA
MEMBERS
CREDIT
UNION

PENNSYLVANIA ST

WABASH ST

CONSOLIDATED
⑪⑤ BUILDING

⑩⑦ CUPS
COFFEE
SHOP

NATIONAL
BANK OF
INDIANAPOLIS
$

BRENNER DESIGN

ONE-
TWENTY
MARKET
SUITES
⑫⓪

KAMELEON

TALBOTT ST

RED BRICK
DANCE STUDIO

⑬⓪½ ⑬⓪
DELAWARE
NEWS CO.

YOUNG & YOUNG
PIZZA

BYRON'S NO-LIMIT BAIL

STARS SANDWICH MKT.

BAIL BONDS
ADVANTAGE

STOCKYARDS
BANK & TRUST

136 EAST
MARKET ST.

⑮⓪

CIRCLE BAR
SALOON

LUKE CAFE
MART

PRINTING
PARTNERS

⑩⑥
SUBWAY

DELAWARE ST

MARKET ST

© 2004 C.A.

TO METHODIST HOSPITAL, CLARIAN HEALTH

MIKE'S EXPRESS CARWASH (1219)

I-65

& M.D. OFFICES, 1 MILE

11TH ST

WTHR CH13 WALV (1000)

(1099) LANDMARK CENTER

10TH ST

☒USPS GATEWAY PLAZA (950)

MIDTOWN COMM. MENTAL HEALTH (96A)
SENIOR APT.
CORNER-STONE CH. (940)

ST JOSEPH ST

SHURGARD STORAGE CENTER (933)

PIERSON

MSKTD & ASSOC. (930)

MERIDIAN ST

(21) RADIO ONE
WTLC AM&FM
WHHH-FM
WYJZ-FM
WDNI-TV

SCIOTO ST

TAYLOR-MADE PIZZA (934)
LIVING RM. LOUNGE
JAGUAR REST. (924)

SAHM ST

TURNVEREIN APTS. (902)

(923) FINISH-MASTER AUTO-MOTIVE PAINT

THE PLAZA

9TH ST

(845) IPD (25)
WELWORTH LOCK CO.

PIERSON ST

DRESS FOR SUCCESS INDPL. (850)
INDIANA BAIL BONDS
MIDTOWN MENTAL HEALTH SERVICES
(802)

AMBASSADOR APARTMENTS

INDIANAPOLIS-MARION COUNTY PUBLIC LIBRARY

(811) LEE'S LIQUORS

ST CLAIR ST

ILLINOIS ST

PENNSYLVANIA ST

© 2004 C.A.

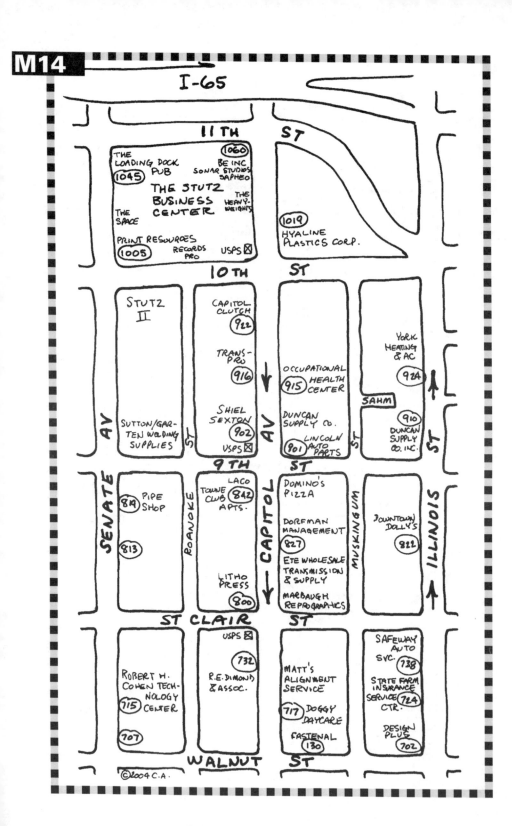

I-65

11TH ST

THE LOADING DOCK PUB 1045
1060 BE INC SONAR STUDIOS BAPHEO
THE STUTZ BUSINESS CENTER
THE HEAVY-WEIGHTS
THE SPACE
PRINT RESOURCES 1005 RECORDS PRO USPS

1019 HYALINE PLASTICS CORP.

10TH ST

STUTZ II
CAPITOL CLUTCH 922
TRANS-PRO 916
SHIEL SEXTON 902 USPS
SUTTON/GARTEN WELDING SUPPLIES
OCCUPATIONAL HEALTH CENTER 915
DUNCAN SUPPLY CO.
LINCOLN AUTO PARTS 801
YORK HEATING & AC 924
SAHM
DUNCAN SUPPLY CO. INC. 910

9TH ST

PIPE SHOP 819
813
LACO TOWNE CLUB APTS. 842
LITHO PRESS 800
DOMINO'S PIZZA
DORFMAN MANAGEMENT 827
ETE WHOLESALE TRANSMISSION & SUPPLY
MARBAUGH REPROGRAPHICS
DOWNTOWN DOLLY'S 822

SENATE AV
ROANOKE ST
CAPITOL AV
MUSKINGUM ST
ILLINOIS ST

ST CLAIR ST

USPS 732
R.E. DIMOND & ASSOC.
ROBERT H. COHEN TECHNOLOGY CENTER 715
707
MATT'S ALIGNMENT SERVICE
DOGGY DAYCARE 717
FASTENAL 130
SAFEWAY AUTO SVC. 738
STATE FARM INSURANCE SERVICE CTR. 724
DESIGN PLUS 702

WALNUT ST

©2004 C.A.

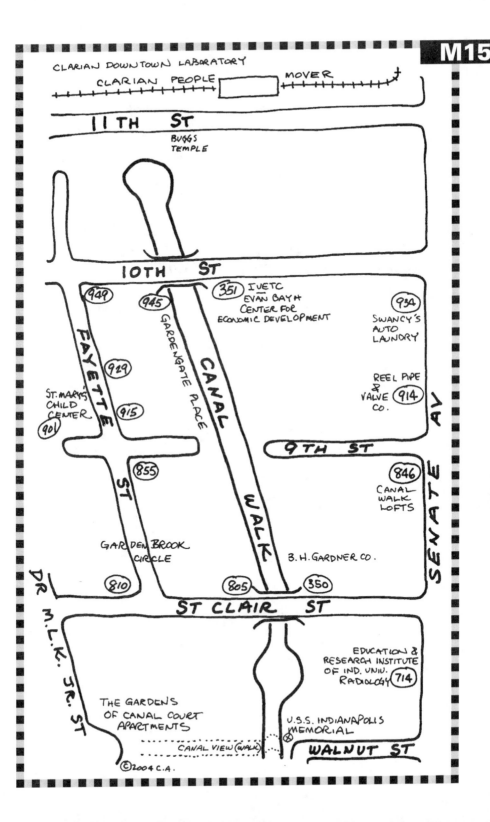

CRISPUS ATTUCKS
MIDDLE SCHOOL
(1140)

CLARIAN PEOPLE MOVER

11TH ST

STARBUCKS ⊠ CHAS. BROWN, ARCH.
USPS→ INDY'S COLLEGE
BOOKSTORE
HOLLYWOOD ▬ FAMILY DOLLAR
VIDEO
HARDEE'S (645) ▬ SAV-A-LOT

10TH ST

DONATO'S PIZZA MAGIA
PIZZA
PAPA (958)
JOHN'S
TACO BELL (941)
& PIZZA GREATER
HUT PIZZA GOTHSEMANE
EXPRESS RANSOM MISS. BAPTIST
BEST TASTE PLACE
CHINESE (901)
(860) SAISAKI GRILL (902)
ADDIE'S SUBWAY 9TH ST
45-MIN. ⊕DOBA MEX.
CLNRS. AU BON
IND. BLDG. PAIN INDIANA (685)
KELLEY ⊠ AV. APTS.
MYERS USPS
KARATE (803)

LOCKEFIELD COMMONS
PACA ST
CAMP ST
CALIFORNIA ST

ST CLAIR ST
(601) GOODWIN PLAZA
(777) INDIANAPOLIS APTS.
BLAKE ST URBAN
LOCKEFIELD LEAGUE ST. PHILIP'S
GARDENS EPISCOPAL
WALKER CHURCH (720)
PLAZA
(718) WILLIS
WALNUT ST UPS MOR-
WALKER TUARY (632)
INDIANA AV CLRY BEAUTY (611)
SALON MADAME
WALKER
THEA-
BLACKFORD ST TRE
CTR.

NORTH ST
IUPUI (550) SIGMA
NORTH ST. IUPUI THETA TAU
GARAGE CABLE CENTER FOR
BLDG NURSING
SCHOOL OF SCHOLARSHIP
INFORMATICS
SCHOOL OF
MUSIC

MICHIGAN ST
© 2004 C.A.

UNIV. BLVD.
DR. MARTIN LUTHER KING JR. ST

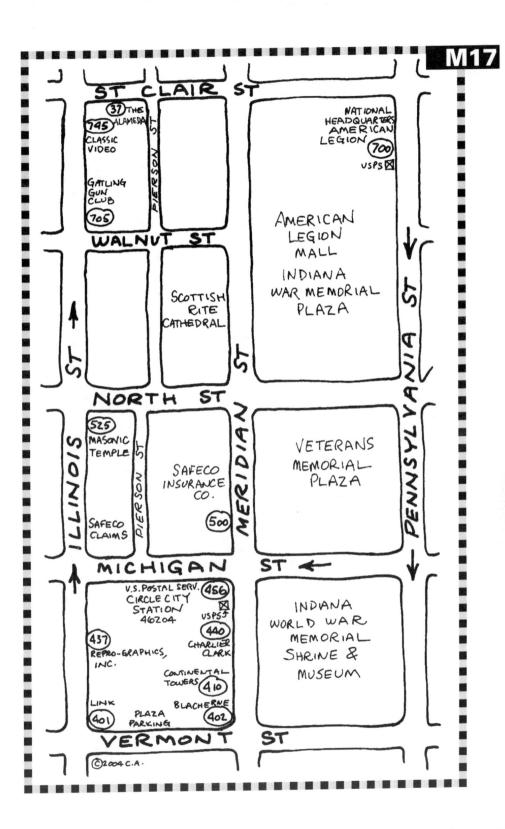

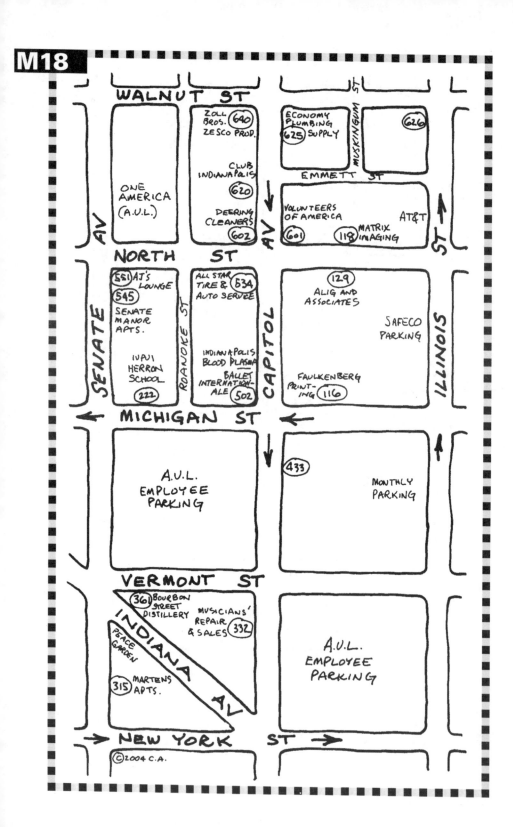

M19

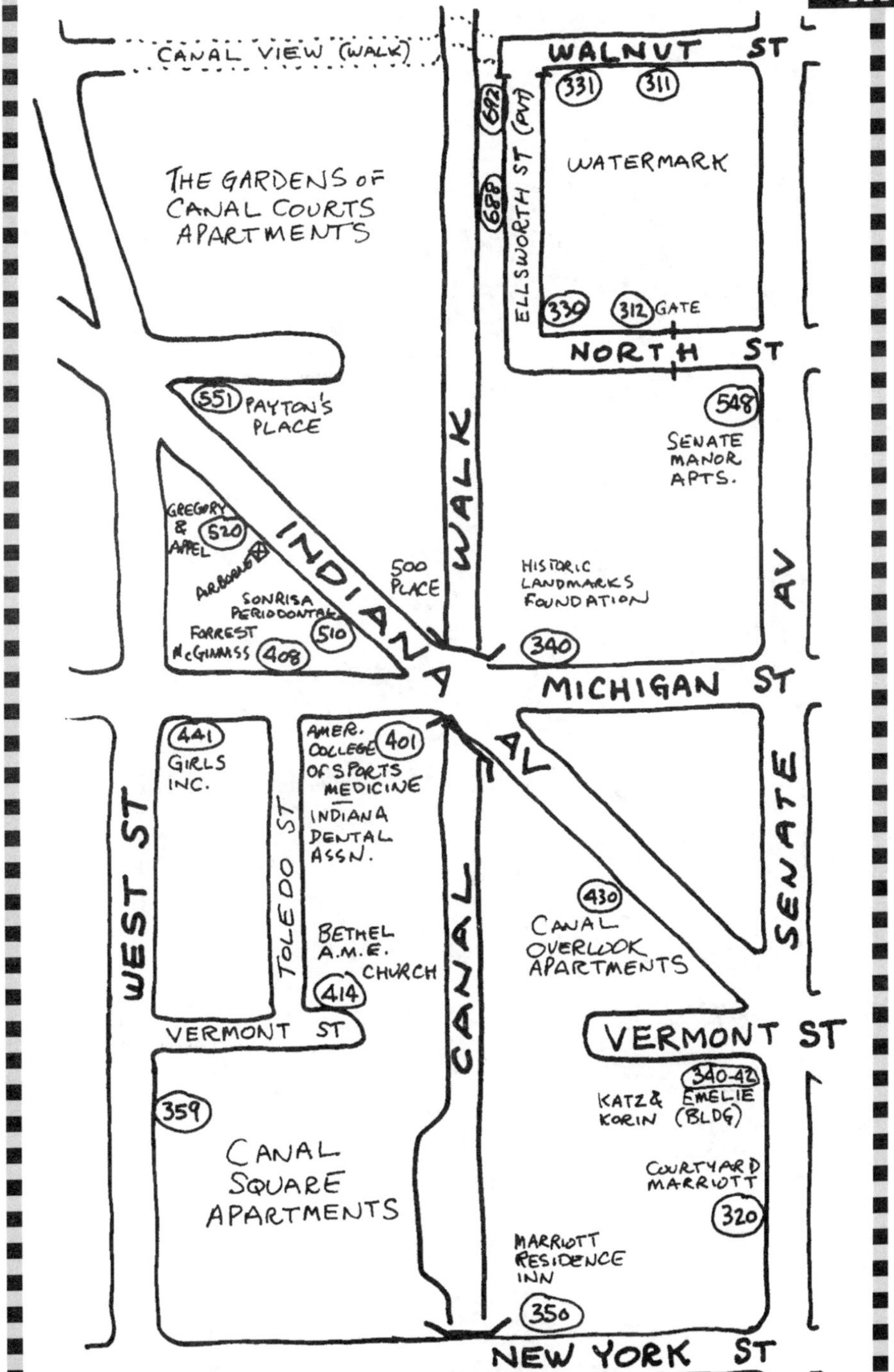
CANAL VIEW (WALK)
WALNUT ST
331
311
692
688
ELLSWORTH ST (PVT)
WATERMARK
330
312
GATE
THE GARDENS OF CANAL COURTS APARTMENTS
NORTH ST
551
PAYTON'S PLACE
548
SENATE MANOR APTS.
GREGORY & APPEL
520
INDIANA
WALK
500 PLACE
HISTORIC LANDMARKS FOUNDATION
SONRISA PERIODONTAL
FORREST McGINNSS
510
408
340
AV
MICHIGAN ST
441
GIRLS INC.
AMER. COLLEGE OF SPORTS MEDICINE
401
INDIANA DENTAL ASSN.
AV
SENATE
WEST ST
TOLEDO ST
430
CANAL OVERLOOK APARTMENTS
BETHEL A.M.E. CHURCH
414
CANAL
VERMONT ST
VERMONT ST
340-42
KATZ & KORIN
EMELIE (BLDG)
359
CANAL SQUARE APARTMENTS
COURTYARD MARRIOTT
320
MARRIOTT RESIDENCE INN
350
NEW YORK ST
©2004 C.A.

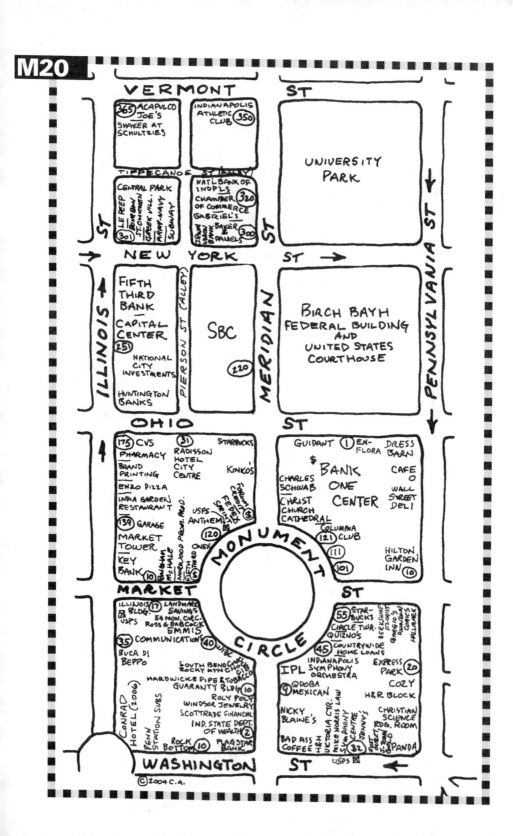

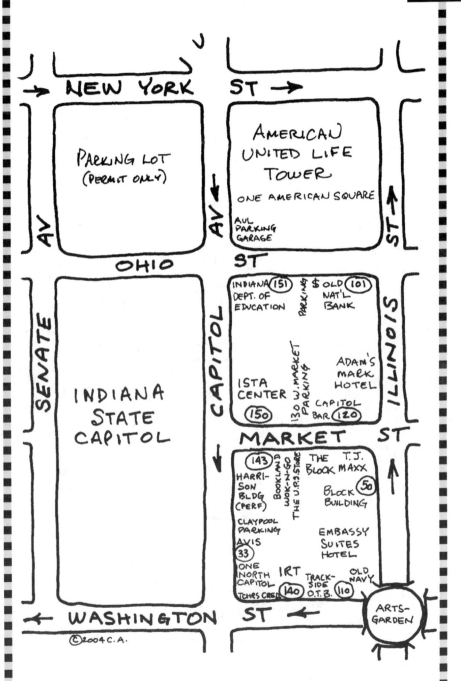

NEW YORK ST →

PARKING LOT (PERMIT ONLY)

AMERICAN UNITED LIFE TOWER

ONE AMERICAN SQUARE

AUL PARKING GARAGE

AV

AV

ILLINOIS ST

OHIO ST

SENATE

INDIANA STATE CAPITOL

CAPITOL

INDIANA DEPT. OF EDUCATION 151

PARKING

$ OLD NAT'L BANK 101

130 W. MARKET PARKING

ISTA CENTER 150

ADAM'S MARK HOTEL

CAPITOL BAR 120

MARKET ST

HARRI-SON BLDG (PERF) 143

BOOKLAND WOK-N-GO THE U.P.S. STORE

THE BLOCK T.J. MAXX

BLOCK BUILDING 50

CLAYPOOL PARKING

AVIS 33

EMBASSY SUITES HOTEL

ONE NORTH CAPITOL IRT

TRACK-SIDE O.T.B. 110

OLD NAVY

TCHRS CRED 140

ARTS-GARDEN

← WASHINGTON ST ←

© 2004 C.A.

NEW YORK ST

INDIANA HISTORICAL SOCIETY

WALK

INDIANA GOVERNMENT CENTER

SENATE AVENUE PARKING FACILITY (STATE EMPLOYEES ONLY)

450

OHIO ST

INDIANAPOLIS FIRE DEPT. STATION NO. 13

WHEEL FUN BOAT RENT.

OHIO ST. BASIN

CANAL

323

INDIANA STATE LIBRARY & HISTORICAL BUILDING

STATE CENTER DAY NURSERY

LAW ENFORCEMENT & FIRE FIGHTERS MEMORIAL

INDIANA GOVERNMENT CTR. NORTH

100

WEST ST

GOVERNMENT PL

INDIANA GOVERNMENT CTR. SOUTH

402

302

SENATE AV

WASHINGTON ST

INDIANA GOVERNMENT CENTER PARKING FACILITY (PUBLIC PARKING)

MISSOURI ST

UNEMPLOYMENT INSURANCE REVIEW BD. 325

OLD TRANSIT BLDG. 309

SUBWAY

LOUGHMILLER'S PUB & EATERY

301

SHULA'S STEAK HOUSE

MARRIOTT HOTEL

CIRCLE CITY BAR & GRILLE

CHAMPION'S SPORTS BAR

350

WESTIN HOTEL

50

(SOUTH CAPITOL)

MARYLAND ST

© 2004 C.A.

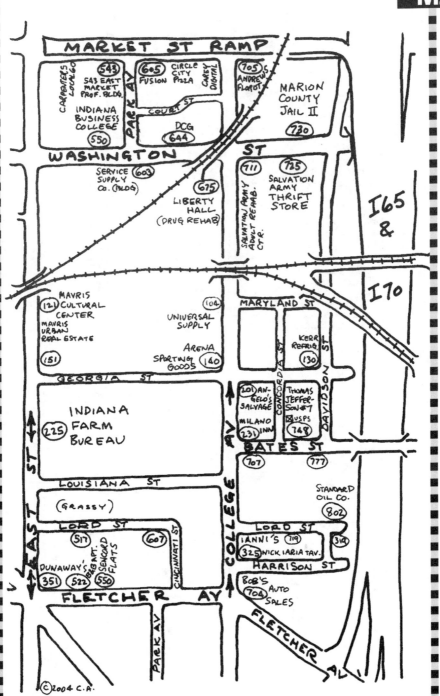

MARKET ST RAMP

CARBONE'S LOCAL 60
543 EAST MARKET PROF. BLDG.
INDIANA BUSINESS COLLEGE
PARK AV
543
605 FUSION
CIRCLE CITY PIZZA
CAREY DENTAL
705 S. ANDREW FLORIST
MARION COUNTY JAIL II

COURT ST
550
DCG
644
730

WASHINGTON ST

SERVICE SUPPLY CO. (BLDG) 603
675
LIBERTY HALL (DRUG REHAB)
711
725
SALVATION ARMY THRIFT STORE
SALVATION ARMY ADULT REHAB. CTR.

I 65 &

I 70

MAVRIS 121 CULTURAL CENTER
MAVRIS URBAN REAL ESTATE
151

104
MARYLAND ST
UNIVERSAL SUPPLY
ARENA SPORTING GOODS 140
KERR REFRIG. 130
DAVIDSON ST

GEORGIA ST

INDIANA FARM BUREAU 225

EAST ST

COLLEGE AV

201 ANGELO'S SALVAGE
MILANO INN 231
CONCORDIA ST
THOMAS JEFFERSON #7
USPS 748
BATES ST
707
777

LOUISIANA ST

(GRASSY)

STANDARD OIL CO.
802

LORD ST
517
607
CINCINNATI ST
LORD ST
IANNI'S 719
325 NICK IARIA TAV.
314

B&B APT. SENIOR FLATS
DUNAWAY'S 351 522 550
HARRISON ST
BOB'S AUTO SALES 704

FLETCHER AV

PARK AV

FLETCHER AL.

© 2004 C.A.

M24

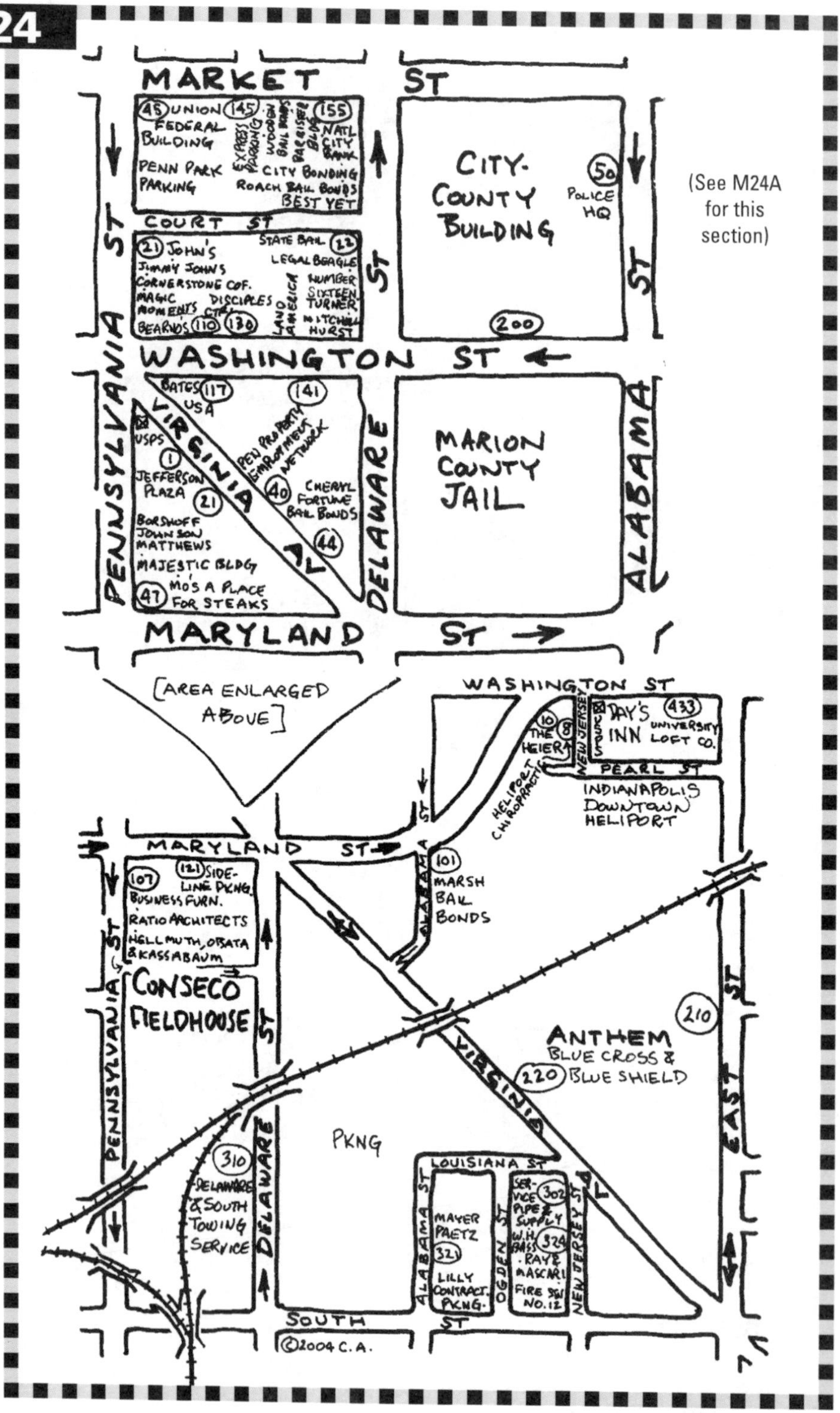
MARKET ST
COURT ST
WASHINGTON ST
MARYLAND ST
PENNSYLVANIA ST
DELAWARE ST
ALABAMA ST
VIRGINIA AV
45 UNION FEDERAL BUILDING
145 EXPRESS PARKING
PENN PARK PARKING
155 NATL CITY BANK
CITY BONDING
ROACH BAIL BONDS
BEST YET
CITY-COUNTY BUILDING
50 POLICE HQ
200
(See M24A for this section)
21 JOHN'S
JIMMY JOHNS
CORNERSTONE COF.
MAGIC MOMENTS
DISCIPLES CTR
BEARNO'S
110
130
LAND AMERICA
STATE BAIL
22
LEGAL BEAGLE
NUMBER SIXTEEN
TURNER
MITCHELL HURST
BATES USA
117
141
USPS
1
JEFFERSON PLAZA
21
BORSHOFF JOHNSON MATTHEWS
MAJESTIC BLDG
47 MO'S A PLACE FOR STEAKS
PEN PROPERTY EMPLOYMENT NETWORK
40
CHERYL FORTUNE BAIL BONDS
44
MARION COUNTY JAIL
[AREA ENLARGED ABOVE]
WASHINGTON ST
10 THE HEIERA
8
NEW JERSEY
DAY'S INN
433 UNIVERSITY LOFT CO.
PEARL ST
INDIANAPOLIS DOWNTOWN HELIPORT
HELIPORT CHIROPRACTIC
MARYLAND ST
107
121 SIDE-LINE PKNG.
BUSINESS FURN.
RATIO ARCHITECTS
HELLMUTH, OBATA & KASSABAUM
101 MARSH BAIL BONDS
CONSECO FIELDHOUSE
PENNSYLVANIA ST
DELAWARE ST
210
ANTHEM BLUE CROSS & BLUE SHIELD
220
EAST ST
VIRGINIA AV
PKNG
310 DELAWARE & SOUTH TOWING SERVICE
LOUISIANA ST
ALABAMA ST
MAYER PAETZ
321
LILLY CONTRACT. PKNG.
OGDEN ST
SERVICE PIPE & SUPPLY
302
W.H. BASS
324
RAY & MASCARI
FIRE STN NO. 12
NEW JERSEY ST
SOUTH ST
©2004 C. A.

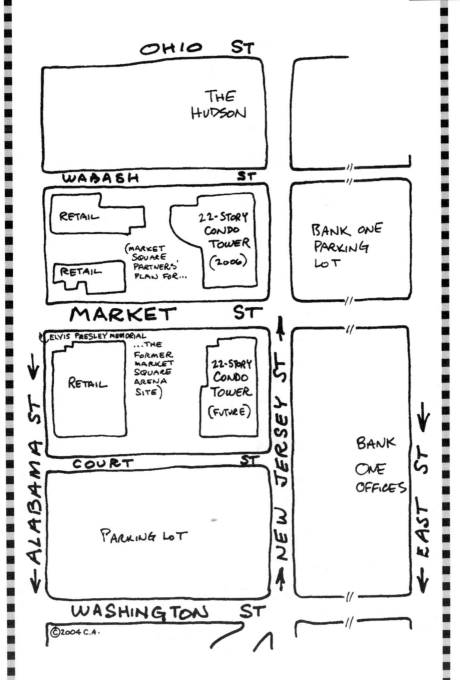

OHIO ST

THE HUDSON

WABASH ST

RETAIL

(MARKET SQUARE PARTNERS' PLAN FOR...

RETAIL

22-STORY CONDO TOWER (2006)

BANK ONE PARKING LOT

MARKET ST

ELVIS PRESLEY MEMORIAL

...THE FORMER MARKET SQUARE ARENA SITE)

RETAIL

22-STORY CONDO TOWER (FUTURE)

COURT ST

PARKING LOT

BANK ONE OFFICES

ALABAMA ST

NEW JERSEY ST

EAST ST

WASHINGTON ST

© 2004 C.A.

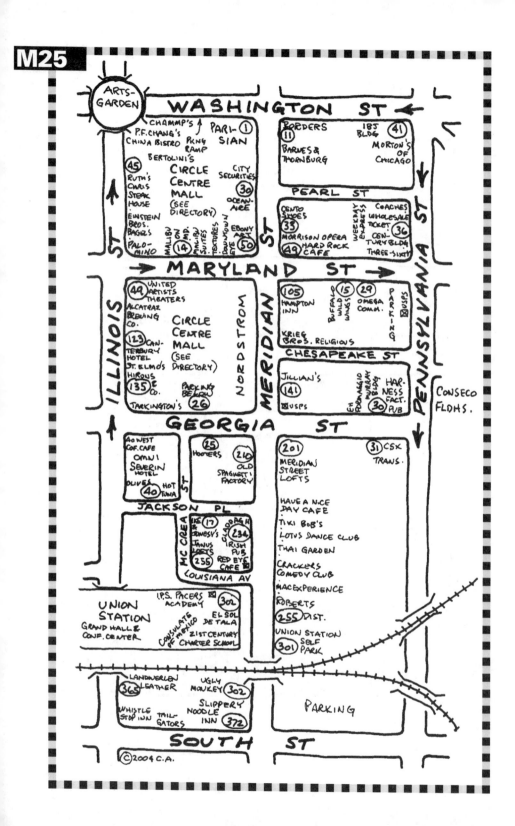

ARTS-GARDEN

WASHINGTON ST

CHAMMP'S PARI- ①
P.F.CHANG'S SIAN
CHINA BISTRO PKNG RAMP

BORDERS 18J BLDG ㊶
⑪
BARNES & THORNBURG MORTON'S OF CHICAGO

BERTOLINI'S
㊺ CIRCLE CENTRE MALL (SEE DIRECTORY)
RUTH'S CHRIS STEAK HOUSE
EINSTEIN BROS. BAGELS
PALO-MINO

CITY SECURITIES
㉚ OCEAN-AIRE

MALIBU ON MD. ⑭ EMBASSY SUITES TEXTURES
DOWNTOWN EYE ⑤⓪ EBONY ART

PEARL ST

CENTO SHOES ㉟
MORRISON OPERA
㊾ HARD ROCK CAFE
WEEKDAY EXPRESS
COACHES WHOLESALE TICKET ㊱ CENTURY BLDG THREE-SIXTY

MARYLAND ST

ILLINOIS ST

㊺ UNITED ARTISTS THEATERS
ALCATRAZ BREWING CO.
CIRCLE CENTRE MALL (SEE DIRECTORY)
⑫③ CANTERBURY HOTEL
ST. ELMO'S
HIROU'S ①③⑤ & CO.
PARKING BELOW
TARKINGTON'S ㉖

NORDSTROM

MERIDIAN ST

⑩⑤ HAMPTON INN
⑮ BUFFALO WILD WINGS ㉙ OMEGA COMM.
PARKING
KRIEG BROS. RELIGIOUS

CHESAPEAKE ST

JILLIAN'S ①④①
⊠USPS
EM FORNAGGIO MURRAY BLDG
㉚ HARNESS FACT. PUB

GEORGIA ST

40 WEST COF. CAFE
OMNI SEVERIN HOTEL
OLIVES ㊵ HOT TUNA

㉕ HOOTERS
㉒⑥ OLD SPAGHETTI FACTORY

② ⓪ ① MERIDIAN STREET LOFTS
㉛ CSX TRANS.

HAVE A NICE DAY CAFE
TIKI BOB'S
LOTUS DANCE CLUB
THAI GARDEN
CRACKERS COMEDY CLUB
MACEXPERIENCE
ROBERTS
②⑤⑤ DIST.

JACKSON PL

MC CREA ST

IKE & JONESY'S ⑰ CLADDAGH IRISH PUB ②③④
JANUS LOFTS ②⑤⑤ RED EYE CAFE

LOUISIANA AV

UNION STATION GRAND HALL & CONF. CENTER

I.P.S. PACERS ACADEMY ⊠ ③⓪②
CONSULATE OF MEXICO
EL SOL DE TALA
21ST CENTURY CHARTER SCHOOL

UNION STATION ③⓪① SELF PARK

CONSECO FLDHS.

LANDWERLEN LEATHER ③⑥⑤
UGLY MONKEY ③⓪②
WHISTLE STOP INN TAIL-GATORS
SLIPPERY NOODLE INN ③⑦②

PARKING

SOUTH ST

© 2004 C.A.

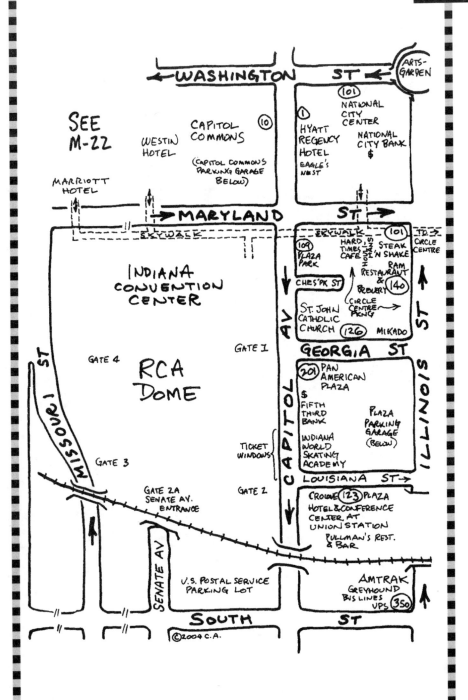

SEE M-22

WASHINGTON ST
ARTS-GARDEN

101 NATIONAL CITY CENTER

WESTIN HOTEL

CAPITOL COMMONS

(CAPITOL COMMONS PARKING GARAGE BELOW)

10

1 HYATT REGENCY HOTEL
EAGLE'S NEST

NATIONAL CITY BANK $

MARRIOTT HOTEL

MARYLAND ST

SKYWALK

SKYWALK 101 TO CIRCLE CENTRE

109 PLAZA PARK

HARD TIMES CAFE
ILLINOIS ST
STEAK 'N SHAKE

RAM RESTAURANT & BREWERY 140

INDIANA CONVENTION CENTER

CHES'PK ST

ST. JOHN CATHOLIC CHURCH

CIRCLE CENTRE PKNG

126 MIKADO

GATE 4

RCA DOME

GATE 1

CAPITOL AV

GEORGIA ST

201 PAN AMERICAN PLAZA

$ FIFTH THIRD BANK

PLAZA PARKING GARAGE (BELOW)

TICKET WINDOWS

INDIANA WORLD SKATING ACADEMY

GATE 3

MISSOURI ST

GATE 2A SENATE AV. ENTRANCE

GATE 2

LOUISIANA ST

CROWNE 123 PLAZA HOTEL & CONFERENCE CENTER AT UNION STATION

PULLMAN'S REST. & BAR

SENATE AV

U.S. POSTAL SERVICE PARKING LOT

AMTRAK GREYHOUND BUS LINES VPS 350

SOUTH ST

©2004 C.A.

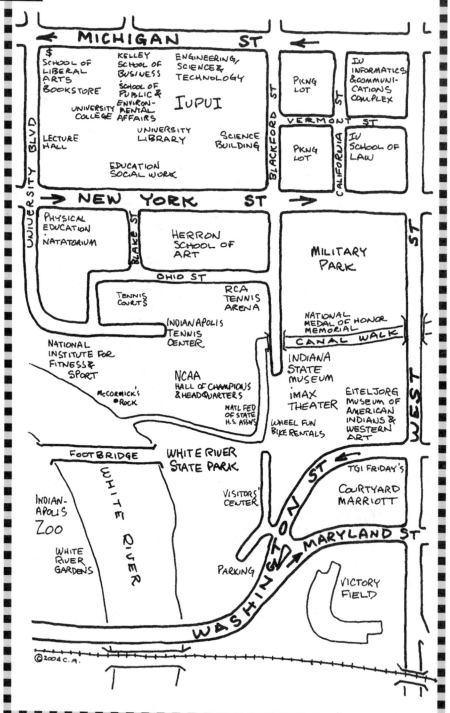

MICHIGAN ST

SCHOOL OF LIBERAL ARTS
$ BOOKSTORE

KELLEY SCHOOL OF BUSINESS

SCHOOL OF PUBLIC & ENVIRON-MENTAL AFFAIRS

UNIVERSITY COLLEGE

ENGINEERING, SCIENCE & TECHNOLOGY

IUPUI

PKNG LOT

IU INFORMATICS & COMMUNI-CATIONS COMPLEX

VERMONT ST

LECTURE HALL

UNIVERSITY LIBRARY

SCIENCE BUILDING

PKNG LOT

IU SCHOOL OF LAW

EDUCATION SOCIAL WORK

UNIVERSITY BLVD

BLACKFORD ST

CALIFORNIA ST

NEW YORK ST

PHYSICAL EDUCATION
NATATORIUM

BLAKE ST

HERRON SCHOOL OF ART

MILITARY PARK

OHIO ST

TENNIS COURTS

RCA TENNIS ARENA

NATIONAL MEDAL OF HONOR MEMORIAL

INDIANAPOLIS TENNIS CENTER

CANAL WALK

WEST ST

NATIONAL INSTITUTE FOR FITNESS & SPORT

NCAA HALL OF CHAMPIONS & HEADQUARTERS

INDIANA STATE MUSEUM

McCORMICK'S ROCK

IMAX THEATER

EITELJORG MUSEUM OF AMERICAN INDIANS & WESTERN ART

NATL FED OF STATE H.S. ASSN'S

WHEEL FUN BIKE RENTALS

FOOTBRIDGE

WHITE RIVER STATE PARK

TGI FRIDAY'S

COURTYARD MARRIOTT

INDIAN-APOLIS ZOO

WHITE RIVER

VISITORS' CENTER

WASHINGTON ST

MARYLAND ST

WHITE RIVER GARDENS

PARKING

VICTORY FIELD

WASHINGTON ST

© 2004 C.A.

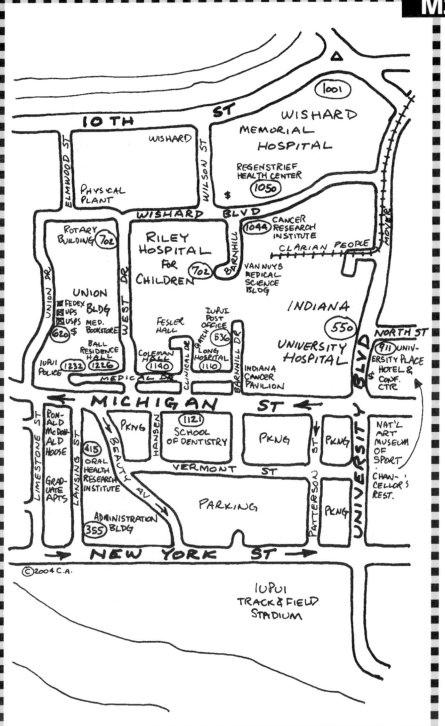

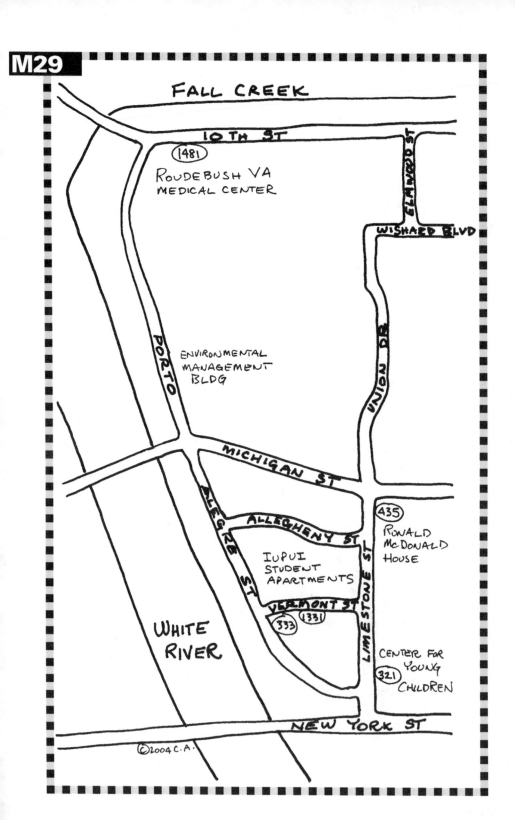

FALL CREEK

10TH ST

1481

ROUDEBUSH VA
MEDICAL CENTER

ELMWOOD ST

WISHARD BLVD

ENVIRONMENTAL
MANAGEMENT
BLDG

PORTO

UNION DR

MICHIGAN ST

ALLEGHENY ST

435

RONALD
McDONALD
HOUSE

ALLEGHENY ST

IUPUI
STUDENT
APARTMENTS

LIMESTONE ST

VERMONT ST

333   1331

WHITE
RIVER

CENTER FOR
YOUNG
CHILDREN

321

NEW YORK ST

© 2004 C.A.

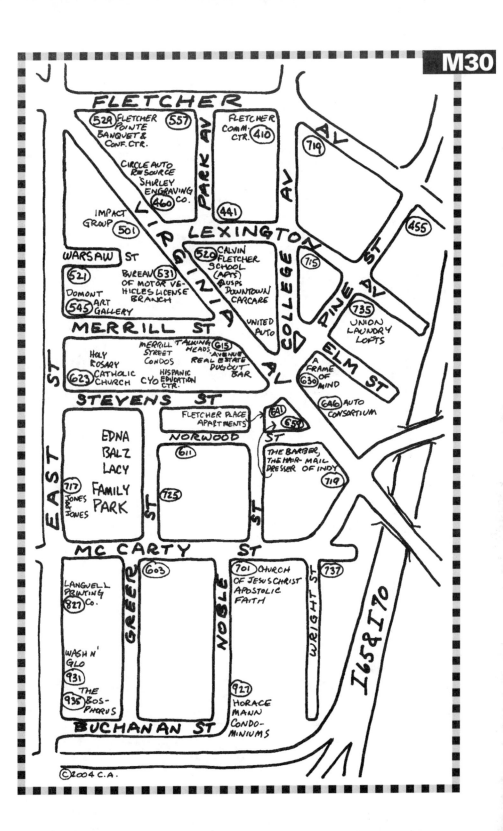

FLETCHER

529 Fletcher Pointe Banquet & Conf. Ctr.

557

Fletcher Comm. Ctr. 410

719 AV

Circle Auto Resource

Shirley Engraving Co. 460

Impact Group 501

441

LEXINGTON AV

715

455

PINE AV

WARSAW St

521

Bureau of Motor Vehicles License Branch 531

520 Calvin Fletcher School (Apts) & USPS Downtown Carcare

735

Union Laundry Lofts

Domont Art Gallery 545

VIRGINIA

United Auto

COLLEGE AV

ELM ST

MERRILL ST

Holy Rosary Catholic Church 623

Merrill Street Condos

Talking Heads, Avenue Real Estate Dugout Bar 615

A Frame of Mind 630

Hispanic CYO Education Ctr.

AL

646 Auto Consortium

STEVENS ST

EAST ST

EDNA BALZ LACY FAMILY PARK

Fletcher Place Apartments

641

659

NORWOOD ST

611

The Barber, The Hair-Mail Dresser of Indy

717 Jones & Jones

GREER ST

725

NOBLE ST

719

MC CARTY ST

603

701 Church of Jesus Christ Apostolic Faith

WRIGHT ST

737

Langwell Printing Co. 827

I65 & I70

Wash N' Glo 931

935 The Bosphorus

927 Horace Mann Condominiums

BUCHANAN ST

M31

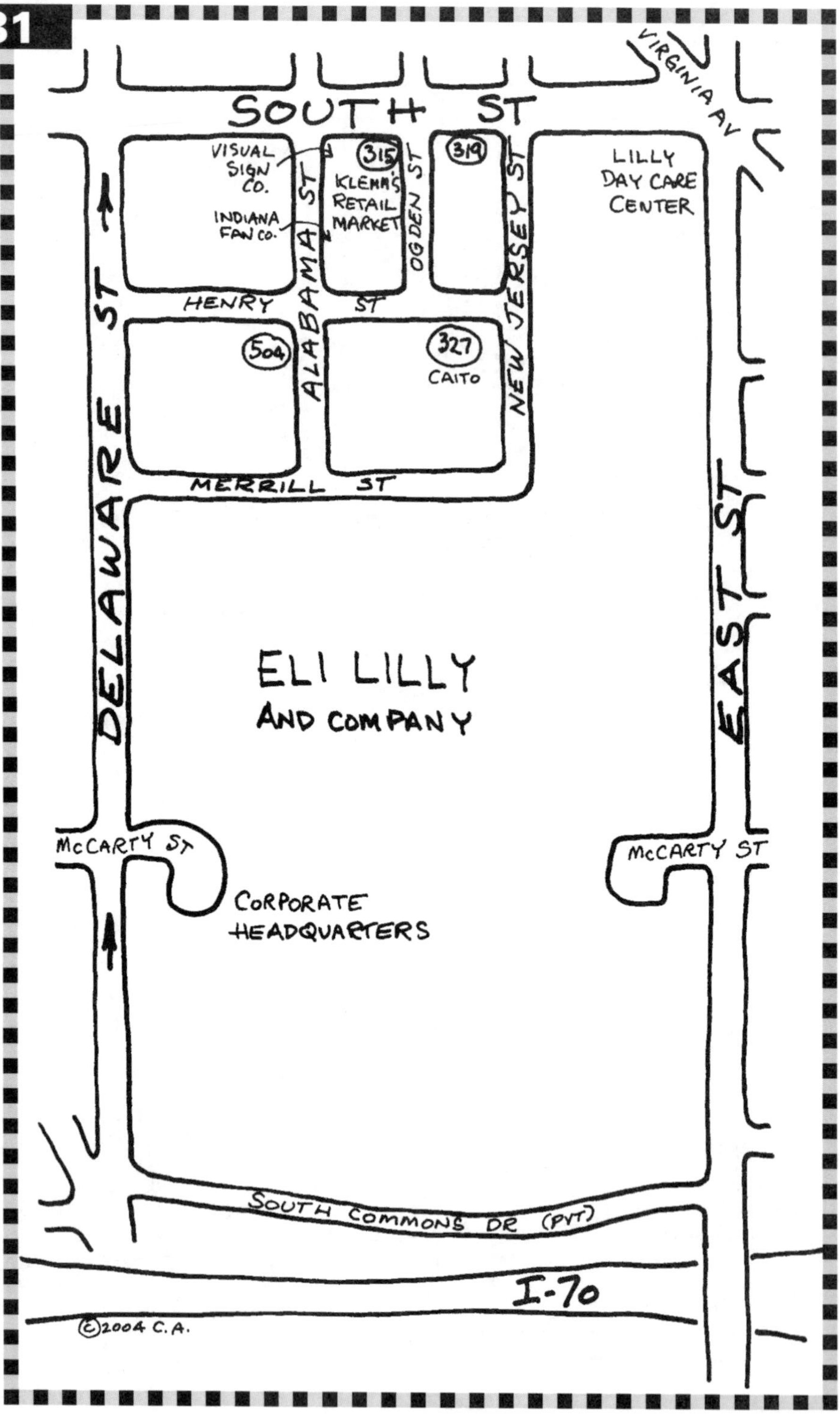
SOUTH ST
VIRGINIA AV
VISUAL SIGN CO.
315
KLEMM'S RETAIL MARKET
INDIANA FAN CO.
319
OGDEN ST
ALABAMA ST
NEW JERSEY ST
LILLY DAY CARE CENTER
HENRY ST
504
327
CAITO
MERRILL ST
DELAWARE ST
EAST ST
ELI LILLY
AND COMPANY
McCARTY ST
McCARTY ST
CORPORATE HEADQUARTERS
SOUTH COMMONS DR (PVT)
I-70
©2004 C.A.

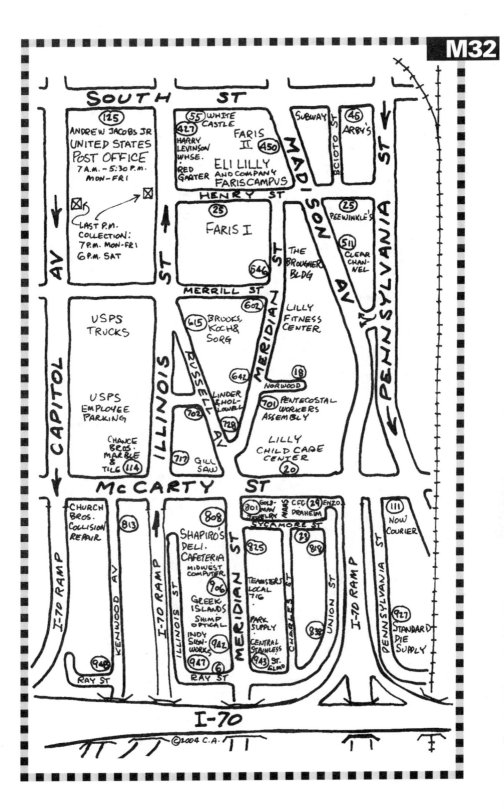

©2004 C.A.

SOUTH ST

419 BASEY'S · RPS
ROAD
HOG SALOON 418

BEST
WESTERN
CITY
CENTRE

EMPIRE ST

CAMBRIDGE
TRANS. 432

PARKING

COMFORT
INN 530
& SUITES

SENATE AV

JOBSITE
SUPPLY

WEST ST

MISSOURI ST

MERRILL ST

601
FULLEN
AUTO &
TRUCK

624
JOBSITE
SUPPLY

MAYER
CHAPEL 448

DEPT. COR-
RECTION'S
WORK REL.

PARKING

INDIANA
CONVENTION
CENTER &
RCA DOME
MARSHALLING
YARD

CAPITOL AV

716

NORWOOD ST

ESKYE.
Com
733
NAT'L
WINE &
SPIRITS

YOUNG
& SONS
412

340

N.K.
HURST
230

SCHERER
INDUSTRIAL
GROUP

AFFORD-
ABLE
BLDG.
SUPP.

McCARTY ST

CHRISTIE MACHINE
INDPLS WELDING

425
WAY-
MIRE'S
820

CHADWICK

415
NAPA
AUTO
PARTS

343
IES

315
INDPLS.
WELDING
SUPPLY

227
CERTIFIED
WELDING
CO.

SENATE ST

234

WYOMING

MISSOURI ST

MEIKEL ST

BABE
DENNY
PARK 918

TAYLOR
&
BLACKBURN

SENATE ST

BETHESDA
MISSIONARY

234

CHURCH ST

943

943

I-70 RAMP

I-70 RAMP

RAY ST

I-70

© 2004 C.A.

RAILROAD

CITIZENS THERMAL ENERGY

(302)

DIAMOND CHAIN CO. (402)

SPEED-WAY

(435) VEE'S DINER

HENRY ST

USPS PKNG. (740) MCI (720) GLOBAL (700) CROSSING

HENRY ST

BUYERS PAPER & SPECIALTY (510) CO.

LEVEL 3 (733) COMMUNICATIONS (701)

W H I T E

KENTUCKY AV

MERRILL ST

AT&T AWS (710)

(551) MAGNETECH INDUSTRIAL SERVICES

MERCURY CAB CO.

DOMINION TELECOM (800) WILLIAMS NETWORK (720)

OLIVER AV

RIVER

(701) CUSTOM FABRICA-TING

SAND ST

WEST ST

KEY LEARNING COMMUNITY

← (777) K-12

WEST ROOFING & BUILDING (602) MATERIALS

McCARTY ST

VACANT FORMER FACTORY SITE

(521) MIKE'S (802) BAR

MARION COUNTY CORONER — INSTITUTE OF FORENSIC SCIENCE

(514) (824)

CRESCENT OIL CO.

WYOMING ST

SCHERER INDUSTRIAL GROUP, INC.

ConAgra Foods

HEBREW NATIONAL KOSHER FOODS

(916)

(940)

(602) IPL HEBREW SUBSTATION

RAY ST

I-70

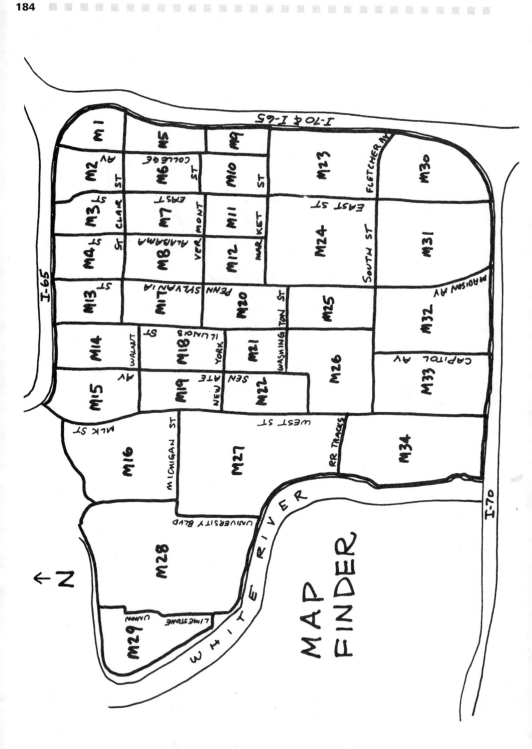

MAP
FINDER